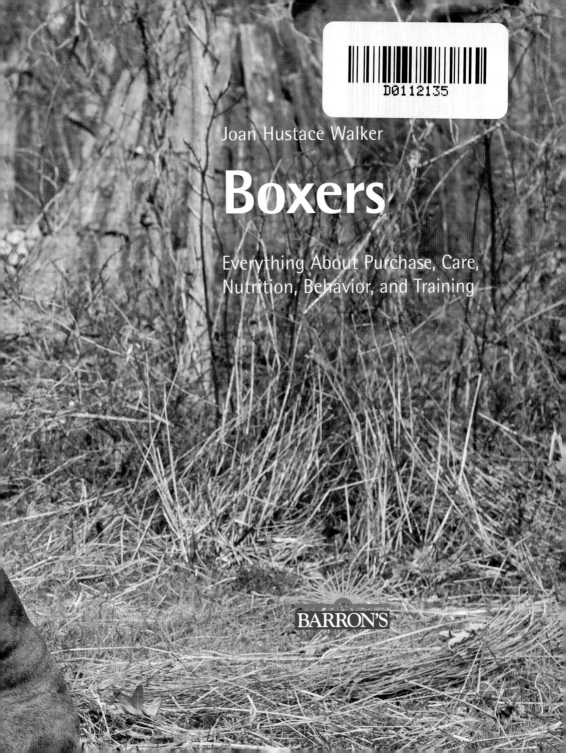

Joan Hustace Walker

Boxers

Everything About Purchase, Care,
Nutrition, Behavior, and Training

BARRON'S

CONTENTS

THE BOXER: A BRIEF HISTORY

The Boxer is a multipurpose, versatile working dog, whose origins can be traced back to the 1700s. Though the Boxer suffered near catastrophic casualties in both World Wars, dedicated breeders in Germany and the United States saved this noble breed and rocketed it into the position of one of the world's perennial favorites.

Early Origins

The Boxer's early predecessor, the Brabanter Bullenbeisser, was developed in Brabant, Belgium, to hunt large game, as well as hold bulls for the sport of bull baiting. ("Bullenbeisser" means "bull biter.") In southern Germany, however, it was popular for nobility to use the Brabanter Bullenbeisser to hunt wild boar. The Brabanter Bullenbeisser's undershot jaw enabled the dog to bite and hold these notably ferocious, easily provoked, and very difficult-to-kill beasts, while still being able to breathe.

In the early 1800s, the Brabanter Bullenbeisser found a new job among the working class as the dog of the local butcher or a cattle dealer's dog. The dog performed the same "grab and hold" function as before but now with cattle. Since the dogs were no longer in the care of a nobleman's gamekeeper (where they were kept in kennels), the Bullenbeisser transitioned to becoming the guardian of his owner's home and a family pet.

Around 1830, it is believed that English Bulldogs (which were much taller than they are today) were crossed with the Bullenbeisser. The English Bulldog is thought to have imparted its white and parti-colored markings to this cross, which is the direct predecessor of today's Boxer.

The Boxer Breed

Boxers have been recognized as a breed in Germany since the mid-1850s; however, it has never been totally understood why a German dog was given an English name. The word "boxer" is of English origin and dates back to the 1600s, with the term being picked up in Germany by the 1700s, and used to mean the same thing: a person who fights with his fists in the sport of boxing.

War Dog Jobs

- **Medic/ambulance dogs:** Boxers were trained to search the battlefield for wounded soldiers and lead medics back to the site of the injured men; the Boxer "Matthias vom Westen," was awarded the Iron Cross for his work as a medic dog.
- **Guard dogs:** In this position, Boxers were often trained to watch for and prevent the silent passing of notes between prisoners of war.
- **Patrol work:** Giving her handler a soft or silent signal, the Boxer would alert her handler to an approaching or hidden enemy.
- **Messenger dogs/couriers:** Boxers were trained to carry messages (without handlers) across battlefields and war-torn terrain.
- **Communications:** Carrying large rolls of telephone or telegraph wire that would unfurl as the Boxer moved between points, Boxers were tasked with important wiring between battlefield points.

The canine Boxer *does* have a unique way of wrapping his forelegs strongly around another dog or person when playing. So, it is possible that the dog was given this name to describe this distinctive maneuver; however, this could be one of the mysteries of the Boxer breed that may never be answered to the satisfaction of many historians.

In 1895, several key Boxer enthusiasts in Munich, Germany, worked together to found the Boxer-Klub e.v. Sitz München (German Boxer Club). A detailed breed standard was developed and approved in 1902, and has varied very little in Germany since that time.

War Service

The Boxer enjoyed great popularity in southern Germany in the early 1900s and was recognized as a versatile working dog with many talents. Unfortunately, these skills were recognized as being useful as a war dog, and thus the Boxer became a part of history when it was the first breed approved for military work in Germany. The year was 1914; the war was World War I.

Some of the finest Boxer kennels in Germany donated their prized Boxers to the government for use as war dogs. Boxers, along with many of Germany's other working breeds, suffered enormous losses. One famous breeder, Philip Stockmann of Vom Dom kennels, took ten trained Boxers with him when the war started, and returned with only one dog, four years later.

For those Boxers that survived World War I, the situation was bleak for years following. Many starved after the war; there wasn't enough food for people much less their beloved pets. Also, many Boxers were sterile. Those that were fertile often produced litters with a high mortality rate among puppies.

German breeders worked hard to keep their cherished dogs alive for the next 15 years. Just when it was hoped that the worst had been overcome, Hitler rose to power and many Boxer breeders recognized that war was imminent.

Boxers in World War II

The buildup of eligible war dogs began in Germany in December 1940. Boxers were tested for their ability to perform certain obedience exercises, tracking, messenger, and protection work. If a dog passed these tests, she was registered with the government for future service.

Passing this test was a double-edged sword, of course. Dogs that were approved for government work were issued ration cards, a highly coveted benefit in a country suffering severe food shortages. Additionally, dogs that received registration were allowed breeding rights, so Boxer breeders needed their dogs to pass the tests in order to breed them. The downside to

The Boxer had one of the highest pass rates, 32 percent, for Germany's military dog ability test prior to World War II. The Airedale was the only breed to have a higher pass rate at 33 percent. During the war, however, the German Shepherd Dog became the preferred breed for military work because of its thick coat and the ability to survive more bitter weather than short-haired breeds.

BOXER FACT

Police Work

The Boxer was one of the original seven breeds determined to be qualified for police work in Germany. The Boxer was approved for police work in Germany in 1921.

having a Boxer registered with the government, of course, was that the dog would be called up for service, and had a high risk of never making it back home alive.

Knowing the losses of Boxers during and after World War I, many German Boxer breeders chose to sell or ship their Boxers out of the country; other breeders who had no place to send their dogs, painfully decided to euthanize their beloved dogs to prevent what seemed to be an inevitable and horrible death on the battlefield.

The losses of Boxers during World War II were equally horrendous in number if not greater than those lost in World War I. The breed served with great loyalty and dedication and often gave its life for its service.

The Boxer in Post-World War II Germany

The years that followed World War II were hard on German breeders and their Boxers alike; however, Boxer fanciers were resolute in reestablishing their versatile breed. By the late 1940s, the economy was improving and the numbers of Boxers was increasing, but German breeders were concerned with the quality of their dogs.

It was during this time that the Boxer-Klub e.v. Sitz München felt the need to emphasize not only correct conformation, but encourage health and temperament testing. The result was the introduction of an optional, breed qualification test called the Zuchttauglichkeitsprüng, or "ZTP."

In 1974, the ZTP became a requirement for breeding. Today, dogs that fail to pass the ZTP are classified as "Zuchtverbot," and are not allowed to breed. If a Zuchtverbot Boxer *is* bred, the puppies are unregisterable. Even if a Boxer has passed the ZTP, breedings are closely monitored by members of the club.

Coming to America

The Boxer has been present in the United States since the turn of the twentieth century. Though it would be decades before the American Boxer Club was founded, owners *could* exhibit their Boxers at dog shows in the early 1900s. Initially, Boxers were shown in the non-sporting group, but this was quickly rectified in 1904 when the breed was placed in the working group by the American Kennel Club.

The following are some important mile markers set by Boxers in the United States:

✔ 1915—The first AKC champion was imported prior to the outbreak of WWI from Frau Stockmann's Vom Dom kennels, and owned by the governor of New York and his wife.

✔ 1920—Interest in Boxers was seen primarily in the Midwest up until the early 1930s, when Boxer fanciers increased across the country. During the 1920s and 1930s, numerous German "Siegers" (champions) were imported from Germany.

✔ 1934—A fawn male, Ch. Sigurd v Dom, was imported from Stockmann's kennels. Sigurd went on to win Best of Breed at the Westminster Kennel Club dog show in 1935, and was a leading sire in the United States for many years.

✔ 1935—The American Boxer Club (ABC) was approved by the AKC as the parent club for the Boxer. The ABC translated a German Boxer standard and adopted this version as the ABC's standard.

✔ 1938—The ABC discovered it translated an erroneous version of the breed standard, and corrected this with the help of Phillip Stockmann, who judged Boxers at the Westminster Kennel Club dog show that year.

✔ 1940s and 1950s—This is the era of the large Boxer kennels. Of particular note is the "Mazelaine" kennels, owned by John Wagner. At one time, Wagner had 80 to 100 Boxers active in his breeding program.

✔ 1947—CH. Warlord Of Mazelaine was the first Boxer to win Best in Show (BIS) at the Westminster Kennel Club dog show. This Boxer was an "American Bred," making his Westminster win an even bigger deal, since most Boxers shown at the time were German imports.

✔ 1949—Another Mazelaine dog won BIS at Westminster: CH. Mazelaine's Zazarac Brandy. This Boxer also racked up 61 BIS before he retired, which is amazing in itself because there weren't nearly as many shows in the 1940s.

✔ 1951—CH. Bang Away Of Sirrah Crest, owned by Dr. R.C. Harris and wife, Phoebe (Sirrah is Harris backwards), won BIS at Westminster, one of 121 BIS wins this amazing Boxer would receive during his career. Bang Away is credited with changing the look of the breed, giving the Boxer a more streamlined look.

Boxer Issues

Within every breed, there is usually some degree of controversy regarding the standard, or the written description that details what a

particular breed should not only look like, but how it should feel, how it should move, and the type of temperament it should display. Only members of the parent club can determine what is allowable in the breed standard, what is considered a fault, and what is considered a disqualification.

Historically, there have been sticking points—or times when members within the club feel very strongly one way or the other regarding an issue—within virtually every breed club in the country. Controversies usually arise when members within the club want to make a change to the existing breed standard. Maybe breeders feel a dog should be smaller, and they want to reduce the height limit in the standards. For other breeds, it may be whether to allow trimming of the coat or to require a breed to be exhibited in a more natural, less manicured coat. Or, perhaps a "new" color pattern (such as merle) has emerged within a breed, and club members are divided as to whether the pattern is natural, or has emerged because

of an outcrossing to another breed. As you might imagine, controversies can divide a breed club.

For the Boxer, the biggest controversies confronting club members have occurred over the past few decades, and involve whether white or check Boxers should be registered, and whether Boxers with natural ears and undocked tails can compete in the show ring.

The White Boxer

The controversy regarding white Boxers is interesting, since early photos of Boxers in Germany show that the majority of Boxers present at that time were pure white or predominantly white with patches of color, called "check." One photo that has been noted, in particular, was taken in 1870 and is of a check Boxer named "Box," who is lying at the feet of his master, 2nd Lt. Burckhardt, a Prussian officer from Hanover, Germany. Sadly, "Box" was killed by a grenade, saving his master's life, in 1871.

As with the German club, the American Boxer Club finds white and check Boxers unacceptable for showing or breeding. In addition to being disqualified from exhibiting in the show ring, these Boxers are believed to have a higher incidence of deafness, and their skin can burn in the sun.

Of course, regardless of color (or lack thereof), a white or check Boxer is 100 percent Boxer. Though it can't be shown in conformation or bred, the white or check Boxer *can* compete in performance events and makes a terrific companion.

Deafness

To date, 89 breeds have been determined to have congenital deafness and the Boxer is one of these breeds. Deafness can occur in any dog, but especially those with white pigmentation. The hearing loss that is experienced in Boxers is believed to be due to a pigment deficiency in the ear and the subsequent loss of sensory hair cells, similar to the type of deafness found in Dalmatians. Boxers with blue eyes may have a higher risk of deafness in the ear that is on the same side as the blue eye.

To ensure that a Boxer is not deaf, it is advisable to have the dog's hearing checked. The test that is used to determine the limits of a dog's hearing is the same that is used to test a baby's hearing: the Brainstem Auditory Evoked Response (BAER) test. The procedure is painless and records the electrical activity of the brain in response to sounds. Boxers adapt well if they have the deafness in only one ear; bilateral deafness (both ears) is harder to overcome but not insurmountable for owners who are dedicated to working with their dogs.

Another famous white Boxer was "Blanka," a bitch that is considered to be one of the foundation bitches of the Boxer breed, and is a sister to "Flocki," a Boxer that was shown in the Munich Dog Show in 1895.

Fast forward to more than 30 years later, in 1925, when the Boxer Klub e.v. Sitz München declared that white and "check" Boxers were unacceptable for registration. The theory behind this proclamation is that the Boxer had proven itself to be a valiant military dog and solid police dog; however, white was a color that could be seen at night.

To maximize the eligible numbers of Boxers available for military and police work, the darker the Boxers needed to be. The color white was briefly accepted again by the Boxer-Klub in the 1930s, and then declared unacceptable again.

Cropping and Docking

The Boxer's ears and tails have been cropped and docked respectively from the inception of the breed. Cropping and docking had a purpose at one time: cropping prevented large game animals, such as wild boar, from tearing the dog's ears; docking prevented an animal, as well as people, from grabbing the dog's tail and neutralizing the dog's attack.

Within more recent times, however, various interest groups have expressed concerns over the necessity of cropping and docking in today's society.

In 1980, several European countries made it illegal to crop ears or to dock tails, and, as a result, Boxers have natural ears and full tails overseas.

In the United States, the ABC revised its breed standard (March 2005) to include the Boxer's natural, drop ears in the standard. This gave owners the option of cropping in the traditional manner or leaving the ears as they are naturally. The ABC did not, however, condone long, natural tails, stating in the most recent standard that "an undocked tail should be severely penalized."

In November 2008, the American Veterinary Medical Association released the following statement: *The AVMA opposes ear cropping and tail docking of dogs when done for cosmetic purposes. The AVMA encourages the elimination of ear cropping and tail docking from breed standards.* To date, the ABC continues to discourage undocked Boxers in the show ring; however, because German imports have natural ears and tails, these Boxers are showing up in the ring. Owners and exhibitors *do* have a choice; cropping and docking will undoubtedly continue to be a hot topic for debate.

In the meantime, as a pet owner, regardless of whether your Boxer is cropped and/or docked or all natural, you will be able to participate in all competitive and noncompetitive events with your Boxer.

The Boxer Today

Though still quite capable of serving as a military and police K9, only a handful of working Boxers continue to be employed as police K9s in patrol and narcotics detection. Where you *will* see Boxers being used is in scent detection, particularly working with volunteers as Search and Rescue (SAR) dogs.

The Boxer continues to be a less hairy/lower shedding choice for service dog programs that train guide dogs for the blind, as well as assistance dogs for people with disabilities. And, the gregarious and intelligent Boxer often makes for a tremendous therapy dog, serving in a variety of different types of facilities.

Of course, perhaps the Boxer's greatest (and most challenging) job is that of an amazing companion. Boxers have been treasured pets for more than a century, and look to continue in this position for years to come, because as anyone who has had the pleasure of befriending a Boxer knows, nothing compares to owning a Boxer.

OWNING A BOXER

The Boxer is a terrific breed and is a good fit for many different owners—but not the best choice for every pet owner. Knowing what the breed's strong points are in addition to what its challenges may be, can help you decide if this is truly the breed for you.

Benefits

The Boxer has been a favorite among pet owners and dog fanciers for more than half a century, and there are many reasons why the Boxer has remained a favorite even as our society has changed. For those who have never owned a Boxer before, the following are some of the breed's greatest strengths.

Low-maintenance Coat

The Boxer's short, smooth coat requires no clipping or trimming to maintain everyday good looks. Bathing needs are minimal, as the coat does not tend to become oily or odorous. Shedding is substantially less than that of the double-coated working breeds. The healthy Boxer has low dander, making it the breed of choice among many service dog organizations for clients who have allergies.

Medium Size

The Boxer is not as large as most working breeds, standing roughly 21 to 25 inches (53–63 cm) at the shoulder, and weighing between 55 to 75 pounds (25–34 kg). On the couch, the Boxer will leave enough space for you and another family member, and if you allow her in your bed, she curls up quite nicely (i.e., the Boxer has a small footprint).

Great Family Dog

The well-bred Boxer's stable temperament and high level of patience make her a top choice for a family with children. Additionally, the Boxer is a friend to everyone in the home; it seems there's enough love to go around for every family member, even those who visit only on occasion, as well as neighbors, friends, and your children's friends.

Athleticism

The Boxer has incredible agility and speed, and is well suited for virtually any dog sport in existence. Boxers routinely excel in agility, rally, obedience, flyball, Schutzhund, tracking, and Search and Rescue, just to name a few activities.

If sporting events aren't your thing, the Boxer is perfectly happy exercising outdoors with you. Walking, hiking, jogging, camping, biking, playing at the beach, lake swimming, boating—whatever you and your family are doing, the Boxer will be an energetic part of your life.

Intelligence

The Boxer is an amazing dog to train. She learns quickly and remembers what you've taught her. She is an outstanding choice for those who want to compete in performance events, but she's also great for owners who want quick learners.

Gorgeous, Gorgeous, Gorgeous

With a strong, muscular frame set beneath a sleek, glossy coat, the Boxer turns heads wherever she goes. Whether fawn, brindle, white, or check, the Boxer is striking. You won't be able to walk down the street unnoticed with a Boxer on the other end of your leash.

Outstanding Watchdog

Without question, you will know if anyone is on your property long before a stranger reaches your front door or fence line. The well-socialized Boxer is also able to turn off the alert system and, when you welcome a friend into your home, the Boxer will follow your lead and greet the person with full Boxer vigor.

Social Canine with Others (Dogs)

With few exceptions, the Boxer is happy to live in a multi-dog family and generally plays well with other dogs. The only caveat to this can be same-sex pairings in the home—particularly two female Boxers. If a Boxer decides she doesn't like the other female dog in the home (and the other dog stands up to the Boxer in retaliation), the result can be a lifelong grudge match that requires constant separation.

Socializes Well with Other Species (Cats)

The Boxer *does* have a high prey/chase drive, but despite this, many Boxers raised with cats live side-by-side quite peacefully. Rescued adult Boxers that have had no known contact with cats often cohabit with feline family members calmly, too.

Highly Entertaining

To live with a Boxer is to enjoy smiling. Though Boxers can look serious and even ferocious to those who don't know them well, behind those penetrating brown eyes is a true sense of humor. These dogs love to clown around and be the center of attention. Remember, if you laugh, you will only be encouraging her.

Loyalty to the Extreme

There's a degree of devotion that the Boxer gives to her owner or family that is exceptional. The Boxer does not have to be raised from a puppy for an owner to experience this affection and loyalty; rescued adult Boxers are exceedingly attached and devoted to their "forever" homes. Many people, once they've experienced the love of a Boxer, quite literally will never own another breed, the relationship is *that* amazing.

Challenges

No breed of dog is perfect. As wonderful as the Boxer is for so many different types of owners and families, these dogs do have certain breed characteristics that some owners may find too challenging.

High Energy Level

Unless a Boxer is given lots of quality exercise, mental stimulation, and training, she will be in constant motion in the home. As a strong, muscular, and powerful dog, a constantly moving Boxer epitomizes the saying, "like a bull in a china shop." She'll blow through dining room chairs and jump sofas in a single bound.

Needs Training

The Boxer *must be trained*; she is too powerful and exuberant not to be trained. Training also establishes and maintains gentle leadership. Without this training, some Boxers will become pushy (not mean, just pushy) and will try to rule the house according to Boxer rules, which you probably won't like.

Climbers and Diggers

Owning an athletic dog has its drawbacks. The combination of extreme athletic ability, a high level of intelligence, and determination, makes the Boxer one of dogdom's top escape artists. Of course, usually the Boxer puts her energies only toward escaping when she's been left alone in the backyard. Or, with an intact, male Boxer, he may have a fervent need to leave the yard if he senses a female in season.

Need Human Companionship

The Boxer was bred to be a close-working dog. She not only wants to be near her master, she also wants to spend as much time with her master as possible. This is a highly commendable quality; however, for some dog owners this translates into a "needy" dog. The Boxer will follow you from room to room, or will position herself at a vantage point where she can observe what multiple family members are doing at the same time. This constant shadowing is distracting to some owners.

Temperament Quirks

Historically, the Boxer has been recognized for her amazingly patient temperament and gentleness toward children. Unfortunately, a growing problem within the breed is that temperaments aren't universally what they used to

be. Aggression, fear, and plain quirkiness are *not* typical characteristics of the well-bred Boxer, but are now a part of this breed among puppies that come from questionable sources.

Health Issues

The Boxer has one of the highest rates of cancers among dog breeds. The Boxer also suffers from a host of diseases that have a proven hereditary (or suspected hereditary) basis. (For more on hereditary diseases of the Boxer, see pages 47–51). As a result, the average lifespan of the Boxer has fallen from 12–14 years to only 8 to 10 years.

Destructiveness

As noted previously, Boxers need daily exercise and lots of it. They need daily mental stimulation, too, and they crave human contact. If any of these needs are not met, the Boxer becomes destructive. A destructive Boxer is a bad, bad thing. She can do a lot of damage to your home and yard in a very short amount of time.

Low Tolerance of Heat and Cold

Because the Boxer is a brachycephalic breed,

she is unable to cool herself as well as a longer-nosed breed. Careful attention must be given to the Boxer if she is working or playing on a hot day. Additionally, the Boxer cannot tolerate severe cold. Her shorthaired coat does not provide her with enough protection when outside for extended periods of time or during periods of inactivity.

Drooling, Messy Eaters and Drinkers

The Boxer can produce significant amounts of drool while waiting for dinner to be served or while watching you eat a sandwich. She also has rather sloppy eating and drinking manners. Food tends to go everywhere, thanks in large part to her undershot jaw. Drinking at the water bowl tends to create a splashing effect and then a trail of water from where she was drinking to where she walked for 5 or more feet past the bowl.

Flatulence

If you're looking for the Miss Manners of dogs, the Boxer wouldn't be at the top of the list. Whether it's because she doesn't metabolize her food as well, or if it's just the way her

Time and Money

A recent study related that the average dog costs its owner well over $13,000 in 13 years. This cost estimate was based on the average expense of a healthy dog's basic needs.

In general, the Boxer tends to be a more expensive-than-average breed to raise and maintain in good health over a lifetime. A few of the breed's more common "extra" needs that make it an above-average expense include the following:

✔ **Dental care:** Boxers suffer from gingival hyperplasia, a disease in which the gums gradually grow over the teeth. In order to delay the onset of this condition, it is important to keep up with regular, veterinary cleaning, which is done under anesthesia. Veterinary teeth cleaning costs a minimum of $200/year, but the worse the teeth are, the more expensive the cleaning.

✔ **Prescription preventives:** The Boxer is a mid-sized dog, so prescriptions that are dosed according to the dog's weight will cost more for the Boxer than for a small-breed dog. Heartworm prevention, which is needed year-round in most areas of the country, will cost $100 or more per year for a Boxer. Compare this to $25 for a small dog.

✔ **Lipomas:** Boxers are prone to lumps and bumps as they age; the majority of these lumps will be benign fatty tumors *but* because the Boxer is at high risk for malignant tumors (Boxers are at highest risk for mast cell tumors or MCT), each new tumor should be aspirated to determine what it is. Cost for a fine needle aspiration is approximately $100, plus whatever your veterinarian's standard office call visit is ($30-$50).

✔ **Chronic conditions:** Boxers are prone to arthritis as they age, and the larger the dog, the more debilitating the condition can be. Arthritis medications are more expensive for the mid-sized Boxer ($75–$150/month) than for small breeds ($25–$50/month), which are less likely to suffer from incapacitating arthritis in the first place because of a lighter body build and less stress on their joints.

✔ **Expensive diagnostics and treatments:** The Boxer suffers from many different types of cancers that can occur at any stage of life. Diagnostics are expensive, costing hundreds and even thousands of dollars just to determine what is wrong. And then, if treatment is possible, chemotherapy, surgery, and pain medications are exceptionally expensive.

metabolism is, the fact remains that most Boxers tend to produce gas.

Is This the Dog for You?

The Boxer is a highly versatile dog that adapts to a variety of different households and lifestyles if its basic needs for exercise, mental stimulation, training, and human contact are met. If you're still trying to determine if the Boxer is the dog for you, be sure to talk with a variety of owners, breeders, *and* Boxer rescue volunteers. In particular, the rescue folks know what it takes to succeed as a Boxer owner, and can give you unbiased insight into pros and cons of this great breed.

FINDING YOUR BOXER

When looking for the perfect Boxer for you and your family, it is important to take the time to research breeders. It's tempting to purchase the first pair of soulful eyes you meet, but if you really want the Boxer that has it all—temperament, health, and conformation—you'll need to know where to look.

Breeders, Breeders Everywhere . . .

The Boxer has been popular in the United States since the end of World War II, and has remained a top choice for pet owners ever since. Prolonged popularity has taken its toll on the Boxer's health and temperament.

The reason for this is that when quality breeders did not have enough puppies to meet the public's growing demand for Boxers, disreputable breeders were more than happy to step in and produce Boxer puppies in great numbers. When a breeder does not take the time or expense to test his or her dogs for hereditary diseases and freely breeds Boxers with poor health or uncertain temperament, the sterling character and robust health of the original Boxer becomes tarnished.

Today there are far more disreputable breeders supplying the public with Boxer puppies than experienced, quality breeders. The good news, however, is that if you are willing to do

your research to find a *good* Boxer breeder (and you are willing to wait for the perfect puppy to be born), you can find quality Boxer breeders throughout the country.

Who Breeds Quality Boxers?

The quality breeder is an *involved* breeder. He or she works to produce the best dogs, and is aiming to hit the Boxer "trifecta" of excellent conformation, health, and temperament with every puppy in every litter. The quality breeder invests time and effort in producing a better Boxer.

The reputable breeder also wants the best homes for his or her puppies, so he or she will be very careful in screening potential buyers. You can expect the good Boxer breeder to be interested in what dogs you've owned in the past (and how they died), your experience and/or your willingness to obedience-train your puppy, what your lifestyle is like, how much time you

will have to raise a Boxer puppy, and what your expectations will be for the new Boxer.

The reason for what might seem like a friendly grilling from a Boxer breeder is that the breeder really truly wants his or her Boxer puppies to succeed in their new homes. In order for this to happen, the breeder needs to make sure that first, you are capable of becoming (or are) a great Boxer owner. Second, the breeder wants to learn everything he or she can about you to make sure that the *right* puppy goes into your home. If you want to compete in agility or are interested in tracking, these activities will take a certain type of Boxer, one that is an eager learner, athletic, and confident, for example. If you are less active and are looking for an active companion, the breeder may look for a slightly calmer, less boisterous, highly social puppy.

In addition, other attributes of a quality Boxer breeder include

✔ **Membership in a national or regional Boxer club and/or an all-breed club:** Membership at all levels shows a dedication to the Boxer breed.

✔ **Participation in conformation (dog shows):** Quality breeders show their dogs in conformation. It is here that it is determined (by many judges over the course of months or years) that a particular Boxer not only meets the breed standards, but is better than most other dogs. Earning a championship is just one of several hurdles a good breeder accomplishes before considering breeding a Boxer to another Boxer.

✔ **Involvement with and support of Boxer Rescue:** Boxers have a huge rescue problem, and it's not just poorly-bred Boxers that find themselves without a home. A responsible breeder will take back a Boxer he or she has bred regardless of the dog's age or the reason the owners must give up the dog. The breeder should also be involved at some level with a local or national rescue. A **Red Flag** is the breeder who believes Boxer Rescue is not their problem.

✔ **Health tests all breeding dogs and can show proof that they are clear of known diseases:** At a minimum, every breeding Boxer should be tested for heart disease (including Boxer cardiomyopathy), hip dysplasia, and should be certified and registered free of eye diseases (annually).

✔ **Freely discusses the health issues of his or her lines:** Every Boxer line has *something* that is unwanted. Cancer is common in Boxers, and many types are thought to have a genetic base. Heart disease has been difficult to control in Boxers; however, with the genetic testing made available in 2009, the ability to eradicate

BOXER FACT

Puppy Age

The youngest age at which a breeder should ever release a puppy is seven weeks. Some breeders will wait to release their puppies at nine weeks (to avoid sending a puppy to a new home during the first fear imprinting stage). If a puppy goes to a new home when he is younger than seven weeks, he often hasn't learned appropriate bite inhibition and may have temperament issues as an adult.

or lessen the prominence of the disease has improved greatly. A quality breeder should track his or her puppies' health well into adulthood, if possible.

✔ **Provides puppies with early socialization:** A huge benefit to purchasing a Boxer puppy from an experienced, reputable breeder is that he or she will spend a lot of time working to socialize the puppies with all sorts of people in the home. The puppies are not kept in a garage or out back in a barn, but rather are whelped and raised in the breeder's home.

✔ **Offers contact information for prior puppy buyers:** The reputable breeder will encourage you to talk to previous puppy buyers. Follow up on this offer. You will be able to find out if these owners have had any issues with their Boxers and how supportive the breeder has been

in helping them resolve any health or behavioral problems.

✔ **Provides a detailed contract:** The contract will clearly describe the terms of the sale. If the puppy is not being sold on a show contract (where you are required to show and, if possible, finish a championship), it is likely that the puppy will be sold with a limited registration (must be spayed or neutered in order to be registered). Additionally, the contract will include the breeder's health guarantee and, if you have to give up the Boxer, the breeder will require you to return the dog to him or her, or involve the breeder in the placement of the dog.

✔ **Invites you to visit with him or her and see his or her dogs:** With a good breeder, you won't even be able to ask this question because he or she will already have invited you out to meet his or her Boxers. It's a win-win situation: you'll be able to see the temperaments, health, and beauty of the breeder's dogs, and he or she will be able to meet you in person and find out exactly what you are looking for in a Boxer, and what type of Boxer will have the greatest chance of success in your home.

How to Find a Great Breeder

It's easy to figure out where *not* to find a good breeder. You won't find one at a flea market. You won't find one advertising in the local paper, or listing puppies for sale on Craigslist. Those tear-off sheets at the grocery store? Nope, not there either.

To find a great Boxer breeder you need to find the clubs, activities, and publications in which good breeders *do* spread the word about upcoming, quality litters. The following are some of the places to start your search that will yield the best results.

• **American Boxer Club (ABC) Breeder Referral.** The ABC provides a free referral service that is available to all people interested in finding a quality Boxer puppy. The easiest way to access this service is to go to the ABC's Web site (see Information, page 92) and click on the topic: Breeder Referral. The ABC will put you in contact with a breeder in your area.

• **United States Boxer Association (USBA).** USBA is a national club that is run in a manner similar to the Boxer Klub e.v. Sitz München, but is located in the United States. If you are interested in a high-drive Boxer to participate in tracking, SAR, obedience, Schutzhund, or any of a variety of performance events, you might contact this club.

• **Regional Boxer clubs.** On the ABC's Web site, you can search for regional Boxer clubs by your state. These clubs are smaller than the ABC, but also have breeder referral services for interested puppy buyers.

• **Local all-breed dog club.** An all-breed dog club is an organization of dog fanciers who show dogs recognized by the AKC. Usually, there are members in the local club who own, show, and breed Boxers—or they know of good breeders in the area or region. To find out if there's an all-breed club in your area, you can search the AKC's Web site (see Resources, page 92) by city and state, or call the AKC's information phone number.

• **Attend a local dog show.** People who show their dogs are interested in bettering the breed, creating a healthier, more handsome Boxer with an outgoing, confident temperament. Boxers draw sizable entries at dog shows, so you'll be able to see the dogs of many different breeders being exhibited at the same show. To find upcoming shows in your area (as well as entry numbers for Boxers and ring times), check the AKC's Web site for listings and/or *www.infodog.com*.

• **Attend a national or regional specialty.** If you want to see hundreds of Boxers in one location, check to see if a national specialty is being held near you. The ABC holds a National Specialty show once a year, usually in the spring. (Dates and locations for each year's show are listed on the ABC's Web site.) Regional specialties can be held at any time during the year and are generally hosted by an area Boxer club.

Magazines (beware which ones!). Many breeders will list their upcoming litters in magazines, but generally not the magazines that you can purchase at the local newsstand, bookstore, or pet supply store. The magazines that reputable breeders are more likely to advertise their litters in are those for other Boxer fanciers, such as the ABC's publication, *The Bulletin*, or other magazines of the "dog fancy,"

such as *Dog News*. Responsible breeders can also be found in online magazines, such as *Boxer Underground*, *Showdog Magazine*, and *Boxer Gallery*.

• **Boxer lists and forums.** The "Boxer Mailing List" and the "ShowBoxer-L" are two popular Internet e-mail lists where you will find experienced Boxer breeders and owners. Also, at *www.Boxerworld.com*, you can join thousands of Boxer fanciers from around the world for discussions, as well as talk to Boxer breeders and trainers in specific forums earmarked for these conversations.

Narrowing Your Choices

As noted, the reputable breeder will want to meet you, so he or she can find out exactly what your expectations for the Boxer are, what your lifestyle and household are like, and then, after watching the puppies and interacting with the litter, the breeder will know which puppy or puppies will be the best fit for you.

If the breeder asks you what your preferences are—or if you find you are looking at a large litter and have a choice among several puppies, the following are some things to consider that may help you with your decision.

Male or Female?

Is there a difference among the sexes? Experienced Boxer breeders feel that males can be exceptionally loving and sweet, which is often a surprise to people who think that female Boxers would be the sweetest. Females, on the other hand, can be a bit more independent than a male Boxer and if she forms a grudge against another Boxer, particularly a female, it may be a lifelong

grudge that requires permanent separation.

Males may mark in the home or try to scale fences to reach females that are in season; neutering usually takes care of these issues. Females come in season once to twice a year; spaying resolves this. Altered Boxers (spayed or neutered) of the opposite sex tend to get along with the fewest problems, so this might be something to consider if you are adding a *second* Boxer to your home.

Plain or Flashy? Fawn or Brindle?

"Plain" Boxers can be fawn or brindle but have very little, if any, white markings. "Flashy" Boxers can also be brindle or fawn dogs, but have white legs, a white chest, a white collar around the neck, and a white blaze. Whether you prefer the beautiful, dark looks of a "plain" Boxer, or striking contrasts of a flashy Boxer, or a puppy that is somewhere in between, is entirely a personal preference.

If you have a definite soft spot for either brindles (dark striping overlaid on fawn) or fawn Boxers, be aware that Boxer breeders often breed for either brindle or fawn, but usually not both. If you prefer one or the other, you will need to find a breeder who shares your color interests.

Pet or Performance?

If you are seeking a Boxer to be highly competitive in obedience, agility, or another performance event, it is important to seek out a breeder whose Boxers compete (and are successful!) in these events. Virtually all Boxers are capable of earning titles in many different performance events; however, if you're interested in blowing away the competition, then you'll want a breeder who *knows* which puppy will have the drives necessary to excel.

Consider the Adult Rescue

Of course, maybe what you really need to decide is: puppy or adult dog? Adult, rescued Boxers have a lot going for them and offer new Boxer owners many advantages. A few of these benefits include

✔ The adult Boxer is a known commodity as far as conformation, size, activity level.

✔ The adult Boxer's health is largely discernible; hereditary diseases and chronic illnesses are generally evident (though not always) in the mature Boxer.

✔ The Boxer is already altered (spay/neuter), on heartworm preventive, and his vaccines are up to date, which greatly reduces your first-year veterinary expenses.

✔ Adult dogs bond quickly with their new forever families (loyalty is not a problem!).

✔ If the Boxer is coming from a Boxer Rescue, the dog's temperament has been tested and evaluated by experienced Boxer fanciers, and the dog is used to living in a home while in foster care.

✔ The adult Boxer can "hold" much longer than an eight-week-old puppy and is much easier to house-train and/or adapt to a home where someone is at work during the day.

✔ The adult Boxer has a longer attention span, learns quickly, and is great fun to train simple commands. The biggest challenge is usually getting the Boxer to walk nicely on a leash (see page 66); however, with special training tools, this can be achieved without any harsh training methods or being dragged around the neighborhood.

Truly, enough good things cannot be said about adopting a Boxer. In addition to knowing exactly what you are getting (puppies are always a bit of a gamble, much more so with some breeders than with others, of course), you are also saving a life. The rescued Boxer seems to know this and many adopters *swear* these saved Boxers spend their whole lives thanking their forever families with incredible love and loyalty.

The Boxer is truly the "breed in need" of help. So, if an adult Boxer might appeal to you, contact a Boxer Rescue in your area and talk to the organization's volunteers. Not only will you save a deserving Boxer's life, but you will enrich yours with a tremendous dog.

BRINGING YOUR NEW BOXER HOME

Providing a safe environment, both inside and outside, is an important part of raising a healthy Boxer.

Boxer-proofing Home and Yard

It sounds like an easy job: create a safe environment for your Boxer puppy or adult. Boxers, however, are extremely inquisitive, amazingly intelligent, and can be doggedly determined to get into things they shouldn't. Remaining one step ahead of your Boxer can be trying at times, but it's not entirely impossible.

The following are some ideas as to how to make common areas of the home, both inside and outside, safe for puppies and new adult dogs.

In the Home

In general, anything you spot on the floor that can be touched will probably end up in your Boxer's mouth. Keep all floors and surfaces very clean, free of clutter, and remove or prevent access to anything that might be dangerous if swallowed, gnawed on, or chewed

through. In addition, the following are some special notes for specific areas in the home.

Kitchen: Behind many cabinet doors and in kitchen drawers are potential dangers to your Boxer, such as toxic chemicals, such as cleaning fluids, detergents, soaps, and polishes. Also, scrubbing sponges and scouring pads can create choking hazards, and, if swallowed, can cause fatal blockages. To keep your Boxer away from kitchen hazards, put baby locks on doors and drawers.

Also, remove all roach hotels, mouse bait, or other poisons or insecticides. Many of these baits and poisons have a sweet smell or attractive taste to them, making them particularly enticing for a Boxer to eat.

Garbage and trash are irresistible to Boxers, so all receptacles for refuse should be kept behind closed and locked cabinets or doors.

Bathrooms: Put a lid on the trash can to prevent ingestion (and potential blockage) from tissues, dental floss, discarded razors, feminine products, etc. Place baby locks on all low cabinet doors: a curious Boxer puppy or adult dog can easily pop open a cabinet door and chew through a plastic lid or container filled with caustic cleaning supplies. Also, be very, very aware of your medications, both prescription and nonprescription. If you *drop* one of your pills accidentally, your Boxer will ingest it immediately. This can be fatal.

Living Room/Family Room

Make sure the floor is clear of toys (there's something about plastic action heroes and dolls that is particularly appealing to the Boxer), stray socks, flip-flops, cell phones, handheld games, TV remotes, and other such items that could easily become choking hazards in the jaws of a chewy Boxer (not to mention *destroyed*).

Home Office

Make sure that all cords and wires with an electric current running through them are covered and cannot be chewed on. Also, be aware of loose office supplies. Retrieve fallen paper clips immediately before your Boxer grabs one. And, if your Boxer likes to chew paper, don't throw sheets with staples still in them into your trash can.

Outdoors

The major areas that you'll need to pay attention to in your backyard are: the fence, vegetation and plants in your yard, and any decks, pools, and/or crawl spaces under the home.

Your fence: Check for loose or rotted boards, or gaps where a puppy could wriggle out. Also, make sure there are no protruding nails or rough boards that could tear your Boxer's skin or injure his eyes.

Toxic plants: In preparing for the arrival of your new Boxer, visit the ASPCA's Animal Poison Control Web site (*www.aspca.org/ pet-care/poison-control/plants/*) for a com-

plete listing of toxic plants and trees. (Remember, puppies don't need to ingest very much to make them very ill.) If you find you have some of these toxic plants in your yard, either remove them or make it impossible for your Boxer to get to them.

Decks and crawl spaces: To prevent your Boxer from getting stuck or injured in the crawl spaces under your home or in the area under your deck, block access to these areas with strong lattice or garden fencing. (Do not use the plastic orange temporary fencing; a Boxer could chew through just enough to get his head caught in the webbing.)

Pools: If you have a pool in your backyard, never allow your Boxer near the pool unless he is supervised. Additionally, train your dog to use the steps to exit the pool. When your pool is covered, invest in a pool cover that is rated to be a "safety cover."

Supplies and Equipment

Most of what you will need for your Boxer's first day home is pretty standard; however, just to make sure that you don't accidentally forget something, here's a checklist:

✔ Crate: The crate should be big enough for the Boxer to stand up, turn around, and lie down. Puppies will require a "small" crate, adolescents and smaller Boxers may fit a "medium," and most adult Boxers will be happy in a "large" crate.

✔ Bedding: Until a Boxer is older and more settled (and won't try to eat or tear up his bedding), pee pads or a layer of newspaper topped with shredded newspaper make for easiest cleanup in

blockages. Try to find toys that are made for heavy chewers and that won't break into pieces.

Your Boxer's First Night

Your Boxer is home and you've done your homework, so the house is safe and free of puppy hazards. Now what? Here are a few tips for making the transition from the breeder's home to yours a smooth one.

Keep It Calm

The first few days are not the time to have a puppy party, or piles of friends and family over. Allow the puppy to get used to everything in your home and yard in a quiet manner and on his schedule. Once he's comfortable and bonded, then you can allow visitors to see him.

Supervise the Puppy

He's not house-trained yet, so make sure you know how you are going to approach your training (see House-training, page 32) and what method of containment you will use. Mistakes generally only happen when *you* aren't looking.

Establish a Routine

Puppies like routines and will adjust more quickly to you, your home, and your lifestyle if you establish a routine as quickly as possible. Ways to do this include feeding your puppy on a regular schedule (evenly space two to three feedings a day), walk him at the same time of day, and begin putting him to bed at the same time each night.

Don't Plan on Sleeping Much

Some Boxer puppies may not cry at all their first night; others may cry a bit. If your puppy

the crate. Outside of the crate, your puppy or adult may enjoy a soft, cushioned dog pad.

✔ Food and water bowls: Stainless steel bowls are light and easy to wash, but ceramic bowls are perfectly acceptable as well.

✔ Collar: A flat buckle or quick-release, snap on collar is good for daily use.

✔ Tags: Put your cell phone number *with area code* on the tag.

✔ Leash: a lightweight, 6-foot (183-cm) leash is a good purchase for puppies and dogs. Refrain from a retractable leash until you've taught your Boxer good leash manners.

✔ Food: To prevent stomach upsets, purchase the same food for your Boxer as he is used to at his breeder's home or the rescue.

✔ Toys: Boxers love to shred stuffed toys and eat the innards, which can cause choking and

is crying, determine the reason for his cries and try to solve the situation. Some of the reasons for a puppy crying may include:

✔ He is cold. Puppies sleep in puppy piles to keep each other warm. Make sure your Boxer puppy has lots of newspaper shreds to snuggle into, or several towels that he can move around and cuddle into. Keep the crate away from any drafts. If it is cold in your home at night, put blankets over the crate to help him keep his space warm.

✔ He is hungry. Puppies eat more frequently than adult dogs and if he skipped a meal in the excitement of his first day home, he might be realizing that he's hungry now. You can offer him a little snack, but try not to feed an entire meal because you want him to get into the habit of a good routine.

✔ He needs to relieve himself. With the excitement of living in a new home, the puppy is stressed, meaning he is metabolizing food and water faster than normal and will need to relieve himself more frequently. Snap on a leash and take him outside to see if he has to "go" and then return him to his crate.

✔ He is lonely. Your Boxer puppy has spent his entire life (as he knows it) with his littermates. You are now his only company. Place his crate next to your bed so he can see you and you can reach down and pet him.

First Night with a Rescued Adult

The first night with a rescued adult Boxer should be handled in a similar manner to bringing home a puppy. It is even more important with the adult dog, however, to give him a chance to acclimate to you and your home quietly and calmly. You don't want to overwhelm him. Allow him to adjust to you and your family on his own time. Introduce him to new people individually, not in a party-type atmosphere.

Once he has bonded to you, he will look to you for confidence when approaching new things or people. If the bond is there, it is much easier to continue your Boxer's socialization with other people and habituation, or getting used to everyday things in your life at home and neighborhood.

Typically, Boxers are very easy to house-train; they do not like to soil their living areas. So, basically, house-training is simply taking what the Boxer does naturally (not soil his own space) and teaching him to expand "his space" until it includes your entire home.

The factors that are included in successful house-training are: space containment, the Boxer's ability to "hold," and a regular schedule.

Space Containment

One of the most popular methods of house-training is to use a crate. If the crate is the proper size, there will be room for the Boxer to stand up, turn around, and lie down comfortably. What you want to avoid is putting a puppy in an adult size crate, in which the puppy can relieve himself in one corner of the crate and sleep comfortably in the other. With this method, you will only put the Boxer in the crate when he has fully relieved himself, but he must not remain in the crate longer than is reasonable to ask him to "hold."

Each time you remove him from the crate, take him immediately to where you want him to relieve himself in the backyard. When he relieves himself, praise him softly and say, "*Go Potty*," or whatever words you'd like to use. Making the association between these words and relieving himself will come in handy when you're in a hurry and need your Boxer to "go *now*" and not sniff around for the perfect spot.

What's a Reasonable Period to "Hold"?

An eight-week-old puppy that is crated during the day should be allowed to relieve himself every two hours. A four- to five-month-old puppy may be allowed to stay in the crate for up to four hours, if he is quiet and calm during this time. (An anxious or stressed puppy will need to relieve himself more frequently.)

Note: An adult dog may be asked to remain crated for up to six hours; however, a dog shouldn't be crated for more than ten hours *total* during a 24-hour period.

Other Options

If you'd like to offer your puppy a little more freedom during the day, you might consider using a combination of a crate and exercise pen. Place the puppy's crate in the exercise pen, and cover the entire floor inside the pen with pee pads. When you see what area the puppy is choosing in which to relieve himself, gradually remove the pee pads in other areas.

When the Boxer gets the hang of this routine, you can expand his world a little, using a second X-pen, or by baby-gating in a small room.

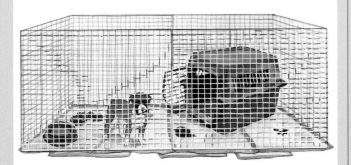

To allow your Boxer more space, place his crate in an exercise pen, covering the floor with pee pads.

Still give him the pee pads in the spot where he prefers to relieve himself.

Schedule for House-training

Consistency is good for the dog and great for house-training. The following is a sample schedule for a young puppy that you can adapt to fit your Boxer's age (by lengthening the containment times) and your schedule (by changing the feeding times, increasing the exercise periods, or revising the overnight schedule).

6 A.M.: Release puppy from crate, allow him to relieve himself; access to fresh water

6:15–6:45 A.M.: Walk puppy

6:45–7 A.M.: Cool-down period for puppy; access to fresh water

7 A.M.: Feed puppy; continued access to fresh water

7:30 A.M.: Allow puppy to relieve himself; contain in room or exercise pen if home and can supervise; crate or crate/X-pen combo if leaving home

9:30 A.M.: Allow puppy to relieve himself; access to water; return to crate

11:30 A.M.: Release puppy from crate, allow him to relieve himself

11:45 A.M.: Feed puppy; continued access to fresh water

12:15 P.M.: Allow puppy to relieve himself again before being put back in supervised room or X-pen, *or* re-crated or put in crate/X-pen combo if leaving home

2:15–2:30 P.M.: Release puppy from crate; allow him to relieve himself; drink water; return to containment area

4:30 P.M.: Release puppy from crate or containment area; allow him to relieve himself; drink water

4:45–5:45 P.M.: Exercise the puppy; followed by playtime; access to fresh water

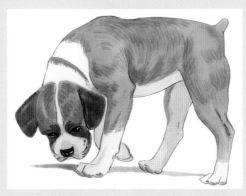

Watch out! The behaviors for voiding include intense sniffing and circling.

5:45–6 P.M.: Cool down period; access to fresh water

6–6:30 P.M.: Feed puppy

6:30 P.M.: Allow puppy to relive himself

6:45–10 P.M.: Supervised time with Boxer; watch for signs that he has to relieve himself

10 P.M.: Final potty break for the night; pull up water

10:30 P.M.: Bedtime

2:30 A.M.: Be prepared to take the puppy out if he becomes restless or asks (barks or whimpers) to be let out

6 A.M.: Time to rise and shine and do it all again!

Body Language

The body language of a Boxer that has to relieve himself is fairly obvious; however, puppies may not know they "have to go" until the last second. So, if you see any of these signs, scoop up your puppy and take him to his place outside.

✔ Sniffing the floor intensely
✔ Circling
✔ Trotting off out of sight
✔ Starting to squat

The Boxer is not a high-maintenance dog when it comes to her daily care and feeding. She has a beautiful, smooth coat that requires minimal care, and she thrives with good nutrition.

Feeding the Puppy

"How much should I feed my puppy?" If you ask your breeder this question when you pick up your puppy, don't be surprised if he or she hems and haws a little as he or she tries to figure out how to answer this question. Young puppies, once they are weaned, are fed from a communal puppy bowl. Everyone in the litter wolfs down as much food as he or she can hold. If you are one of the first owners to pick up your puppy, the breeder may have only a general idea of how much the puppy is eating. If the puppy is the last one to be picked up, the breeder may be able to tell you exactly "3/4 cup of puppy food XYZ, three times a day."

Figuring Out How Much

If there's a question as to how much your puppy is eating, don't worry—there's a simple solution. At your puppy's regular feeding time, measure out 1½ cups of puppy food and put it in her bowl. Do not mix the food with any canned food or other ingredients at this time that might cause the puppy to overeat.

Allow your puppy access to the dry food for 30 minutes and then pick it up. Measure what is left to calculate how much food she's eaten. Measure and feed your puppy for two or more days until you know how much she is eating. Voila! *This* is the amount to serve your puppy.

As your puppy grows, you can increase the amount of food she eats. Your best guide as to whether she is getting too much food, not enough, or just the right amount is to keep an eye on her body fat. A lean, healthy puppy will have just enough fat to cover her ribs while she is at rest. A fat puppy will lose her waistline, when viewed from overhead. A thin puppy will have the last rib showing just under the skin.

If you have any questions as to whether you are feeding your puppy too much or not enough, take clear photos of your puppy from the side and overhead and e-mail them to your breeder. Or, ask your veterinarian at your next appointment—or if you are attending training classes, ask your trainer for his or her opinion. Most experienced dog folks will be more than happy to help you determine your puppy's best body weight.

What to Feed?

Feed your Boxer puppy the same food that she received at the breeder's home. She likes the food, she is thriving on the food, and you know she will eat it. Also, if you make a sudden change in her diet, it will likely cause her intestinal upset, which wreaks havoc with early house-training efforts.

If you want to switch to another brand of food, that's okay. Make the switch over a period of four to five days, and make sure the food is of the highest quality. Cheap ingredients have been

Dry, Wet, or Semi-moist?

It used to be that once you fed a dog canned dog food, she never wanted to eat kibble again. Now, dry foods are so palatable that this is no longer the case. What you feed is more personal preference; however, be aware that canned foods are generally more expensive to feed than dry foods, and don't provide the teeth cleaning benefits of hard kibble. Semi-moist foods are packaged similarly to dry foods but are a bit chewier and some Boxers do not produce firm stools while on this type of food.

known to irritate the Boxer's gastrointestinal system or trigger food allergies over time.

So, how can you tell if a food is high quality or just expensive? First, look at the label. The food should not only meet the minimum nutritional requirements for "growth" set by the Association of American Feed Control Officials (AAFCO) but should also have passed feeding trials.

The food packaging should state: "Animal feeding tests using AAFCO procedures substantiate that ABC Puppy Food provides complete and balanced nutrition for growth." This shows that the nutrients in the food are not appropriate for this age group of dogs, but are digestible *and* the food is palatable.

Ingredients

Another tip for finding a quality puppy food is to look at the ingredients on the label, which are listed in order of weight in the food. The first ingredient should be a high-grade meat, poultry, or fish; avoid products that list animal by-products, as these include parts of the animal other than meat (i.e., heart, liver, spleen,

etc.). Another good choice is a food with a highly digestible grain, such as oatmeal, barley, and/or brown rice; avoid foods that use ground corn or wheat, which are not highly digestible and can be tough on a puppy's digestive system.

Farther down the ingredient list, you might find egg; this is a high-quality protein source. And, you might see some more unusual ingredients, such as blueberry pomace, sweet potatoes, and carrots, which are rich in antioxidants. Avoid foods that have artificial colors, flavors, or preservatives.

Nutrition for the Adult Dog

The guidelines for selecting a quality adult dog food are very similar to those with puppy food. When looking at labels, you'll want to see that the food has passed the requirements for feeding trials as set by the AAFCO for adult dogs. The label will read: "Animal feeding tests using AAFCO procedures substantiate that ABC Dog Food provides complete and balanced nutrition for maintenance."

Except for some high-performance adult dog foods, the average high-quality dog food has fewer calories per ounce than puppy foods. If you are feeding an adult food to a puppy, you may find that as your puppy ages, she will need less food.

If you've adopted a rescued adult dog, the rescue organization or shelter *should* be able to tell you how much they are feeding your Boxer. She may be eating more than she will in three months because she was very thin and needed to put on weight, or it is possible that she is on a reduced diet to shed excess pounds.

You will find that over the years with your Boxer, you will be varying the amount you feed according to the quality of the food, her lifestage, and her activity level. The same Boxer may require three cups of high-quality food a day as a young dog, but require only 2¼ cups of the same high-quality food when she is six years old.

Be forewarned, too, that many pet food labels give a high-end range (based on the dog's current rate) as to what to feed your Boxer. Often, if a Boxer is actually fed four to five cups of food (as per the label's recommendations), you will soon have a 90-pound (41 kg) Boxer that should weigh only 60 pounds (27 kg)!

Homemade Diets

If you have the time, money, and determination to prepare fresh food for your Boxer, you might consider a homemade diet. This diet does *not* have to be raw; in fact, many top veterinary nutritionists do not recommend a raw diet. Rather, the experts recommend a balanced diet.

Balancing a homemade diet can be very difficult. Ingredients must be measured very carefully. In fact, the largest problem with homemade diets is that owners make substitutions or omit ingredients, creating a dangerously unbalanced diet.

If you're interested in creating a diet for your Boxer, ask your veterinarian for a recipe. These recipes are developed by veterinary nutritionists and must be followed to the letter. If you prefer to have more flexibility or variety in the meals you prepare for your dog, you may also be interested in the Web site: *www.balanceit.com*. For a small fee, you can enter your dog's information and create a nutritionally balanced diet, choosing from a list of options in proteins, vegetables, and grains. The recipe will include the precise proportions of supplements that are needed, too.

Basic Grooming Skills

If you wanted a no-fuss dog, the Boxer is definitely a great choice. Brush her out, wash her occasionally, trim her nails, and keep her teeth clean, and you've got a great-looking Boxer.

Brushing

The Boxer has a single, shorthaired coat, so you don't have an undercoat to worry about; however, Boxers *do* shed. To keep as few hairs as possible from lodging in upholstery or on your carpets and floors, brush the Boxer once or twice a week with a curry brush or Zoom Groom. These brushes are made of rubber and have rubber bristles. Rub the Boxer gently in a counterclockwise motion all over her body. This will help to dislodge shedding hairs, as well as stimulate your dog's skin. Follow with a soft, natural-haired brush, or wipe down with a damp cloth or chamois. And that's it.

You can complete your grooming session by wiping your Boxer's eyes gently with a damp cotton ball to remove any residue. To clean your Boxer's ears, use another cotton ball that has been dampened with an ear cleanser/drying solution and wipe out all reachable surfaces.

Bathing

Though the Boxer's coat can be maintained nicely for *months* with regular brushing, it's important to "practice" bathing with your puppy. If you wait for months before you wash your Boxer, it is quite possible that she won't be too fond of baths, and a major struggle might ensue.

When bathing, choose a gentle shampoo. There are many products available, ranging from moisturizing shampoos to those with oatmeal and tea tree extracts, and all are specially formulated for use with dogs.

When bathing your Boxer, here are some special tips:

✔ Put a rubber mat in the bathtub to help your Boxer feel more secure, and keep her from slipping.

✔ Use warm water to bathe and rinse, never cold or cool water.

✔ When shampooing, use a rubber brush or Zoom Groom to loosen hair and massage the soap into her coat.

✔ Shampoo once and then rinse *twice*, paying special attention to prevent soap residue on paws and legs that can cause itching and irritation when it dries.

✔ If you bathe your Boxer more frequently than once a month, be sure to finish with a moisturizing conditioner (and rinse twice), to keep from drying out her coat.

✔ After rinsing her thoroughly, dry her as completely as possible with towels. To keep her from getting chilled after her bath, allow her to curl up in her crate with more dry towels in a draft-free, warm location in your home.

Nail Trimming

Trimming a dog's nails seems to be the bane of dog ownership. No one—dog or owner—particularly enjoys this task. And, because it's a task that is done infrequently, puppies often grow into adult dogs that have had their nails clipped only two or three times, and hate it.

If you have a Boxer puppy, practice trimming nails daily, if you can. You don't have to actually cut any of the nails—just practice holding your puppy's paws and placing the clippers over the nail. Then, once every two or three weeks, clip your puppy's nails. Ideally, the nails should be short enough that when your Boxer walks across a hard surface, you don't hear any clicking.

Dental Care

As a breed, the Boxer does not have good teeth. In addition to being susceptible to the normal buildup of plaque and tarter that causes gingivitis and tooth decay, the Boxer is prone to developing gingival hyperplasia, a condition in which the gums grow over the dog's teeth.

Gingivitis and tooth loss can be prevented with excellent dental care; gingival hyperplasia cannot be stopped, but it can be slowed to the point where it is never a concern to your aging Boxer's health.

Your Boxer's dental care should include the following.

Daily brushing: Using a toothbrush and *canine* toothpaste, brush the outside of her teeth gently down to the gum line every day. Do not use a human toothpaste because it contains chemicals that are harmful if swallowed. (Boxers are smart, but they can't be trained to spit.)

Dental approved snacks: Look for chewies, snacks, and treats that have the Veterinary Oral

Avoiding the Quick

If you happen to cut the tip of the toenail back too far and knick the quick, it will bleed furiously and takes forever to stop. The slightest bump on the nail (for seemingly hours later) will get the bleeding started again.

To stop a bleeding toenail, invest in Quik-stop powder or a similar product for dog toenails that stops bleeding quickly.

To avoid this situation, just don't cut the nail back so far, which is easier said than done, of course. If your Boxer has white paws, she likely has clear nails. If you look closely at the nails, you can see the pink quick. Clip as closely to this quick as possible without touching it, of course.

With a dark nail, you can take your chances and cut the same distance from the tip as you do for the clear ones. Or, if you're not feeling lucky, you can look at the bottom of the nail. You will see an oval shape and then the tip of the nail. The oval shape indicates where the quick is. You can trim safely just past this point.

Health Council (VOHC) seal of approval. These products have been proven to be effective in controlling plaque and/or calculus deposits in dogs.

Annual veterinary cleaning: Your Boxer will require annual cleaning to help her teeth stay as healthy as possible. The procedure is performed by your veterinarian while the Boxer is under anesthesia.

Hopefully, your Boxer will never become injured or seriously ill. It helps, however, to be prepared by knowing when you have an emergency on your hands, and what you can do to help your Boxer.

The following are some of the most common situations in which owners often question, "Is it serious?" In general, a good rule to live by is if you have a question, it most likely *is* serious and requires veterinary attention. Don't put off getting help today for what could be fatal if left to tomorrow.

Diarrhea, Loose Stools

Did you feed your Boxer something different? A new food? Table scraps? Or, could she have gotten into the garbage? If you know she ate something different (but not deadly) *and* she is acting normal otherwise (active, alert, energetic), keep your Boxer hydrated and give her a meal or two of equal parts of cooked white rice and baked chicken.

If your Boxer is a puppy, diarrhea is an early sign of several potentially lethal diseases; see your veterinarian immediately. If your Boxer (puppy or adult) has blood in her stools, has no appetite, is lethargic, and/or begins vomiting, *this is an emergency.*

Drooling

Inspect your Boxer's mouth. An acute onset of profuse drooling may indicate that something is lodged in her teeth or gums. Drooling is also a sign of a bitter taste, which could be from a toxic plant or chemical—*this is an emergency.*

Eye Irritation

If your Boxer is rubbing or scratching her eyes, or if an eye is red, painful, or swollen, it is important to see a veterinarian immediately. You can try to wash the eye with sterile eyewash, but the Boxer's rubbing and scratching can make the situation worse very quickly.

Facial Swelling

This is usually a sign of an allergic reaction and *is an emergency.* Your veterinarian may advise giving your Boxer diphenhydramine (Benedryl), which will be dosed as a mg/pound body weight dose, prior to arriving at the veterinary clinic.

Heatstroke

This is *a life-threatening emergency* and one that Boxers, as a brachycephalic breed with *lots* of energy, are much more predisposed to. Symptoms of heatstroke are excessive panting (dog can't cool herself down), a temperature of 105°F (40.5°C) or higher, bright red tongue, weakness, dizziness, vomiting, diarrhea,

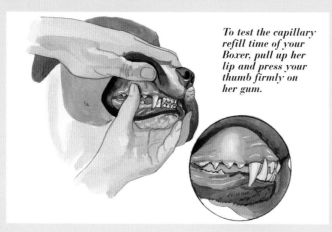

To test the capillary refill time of your Boxer, pull up her lip and press your thumb firmly on her gum.

progressing to shock and coma. If your Boxer is overheated, move her to a cool location immediately with a fan, encourage her to drink water, and wet her with cool *but not cold* water. Check her temperature every five minutes until it is 103°F (39.4°C). Hopefully, you are at your veterinarian's office by then for further treatment.

Vomiting

A puppy or dog may vomit for a variety of reasons, and many of them are not emergencies. Most commonly, a Boxer may eat a bit too quickly and regurgitate her food. (She'll usually eat the regurgitation immediately.) There are times when vomiting is an emergency, however. The following are times when a trip to the emergency clinic is necessary:

✔ Presence of blood in the vomit
✔ Unproductive attempts at vomiting
✔ Swollen abdomen or an overall bloated appearance
✔ Signs that your Boxer is in pain
✔ Diarrhea with the vomiting
✔ Lethargy
✔ Pale gums
✔ Fever
✔ *A puppy or dog that is not fully vaccinated*
✔ *A puppy or dog that may have eaten something toxic*

Emergency Care Procedures

Checking for blood circulation (capillary refill time): Pull your Boxer's lips up and press your thumb *hard* against her gums. The color should pale under pressure and then return immediately (within 1.5 seconds) to a normal pink-red color. Failure to return to full color indicates the Boxer is going into shock, or if certain heart diseases are present.

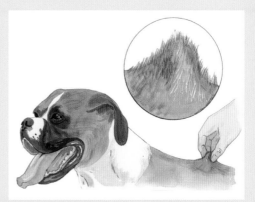

Test for dehydration by firmly pinching the skin between your Boxer's shoulder blades. If your Boxer is dehydrated, the skin will continue to stand up.

Taking temperature: Using a soft-tip thermometer, put your fingers one inch from the end and insert *no farther*. A normal temperature is between 100.5 and 102.5°F (37.8–39°C).

Controlling bleeding: For all areas of bleeding, apply firm pressure. If the bleeding doesn't stop within a few minutes, it is highly likely that stitches are needed.

A heavy Boxer can be lifted by sliding her onto a sturdy towel or blanket and carrying her to the car.

BOXER HEALTH

Preventive health care can do much to keep your Boxer healthy; however, the Boxer is predisposed to several diseases, many of which are hereditary. For this reason, it is important that owners know not only what diseases and conditions can be prevented through good veterinary care, but also what diseases are most likely to affect the Boxer as he ages and what your treatment options are.

Vaccinations

Perhaps the most important step you can take to protect your Boxer puppy against disease is to make sure he is vaccinated. Adult Boxers should remain current on key vaccinations as well.

How Vaccinations Work

If a puppy's mother has been fully vaccinated against multiple diseases, she carries antibodies that initiate the destruction of specific viruses or bacteria that enter her body. When a puppy is born and nurses, he receives temporary immunity from the same diseases as his mother.

The purpose of a vaccination is to stimulate the puppy's immune system to produce his own, long-lasting antibodies.

If the puppy is vaccinated for disease while he retains his mother's immunities, however, the puppy will not produce any of his own antibodies. The mother's immunity is thought to be present in 75 percent of puppies at six weeks, 25 percent of puppies at nine weeks, and a very few puppies at 12 weeks. So if a puppy's vaccinations are first given at six weeks, the vaccinations will be effective in roughly 25 percent of the puppies.

For this reason, a *series* of vaccinations (usually spaced three weeks apart) is given to the puppy in an attempt to get the puppy to produce his own antibodies the moment his mother's antibodies are no longer effective. It's a bit of a guessing game as to when the window of opportunity becomes available, and this is why your veterinarian may recommend limiting your puppy's exposure to other dogs or high-traffic areas until after he has received his second or even third set of vaccinations.

Core Vaccinations

Canine vaccinations are divided into two categories: "core" and "noncore" vaccines. Core vaccinations are those that protect a puppy or dog from potentially fatal viruses that are commonly found in most areas of the country, and are highly contagious. Core vaccinations include protection against:

• **Canine Distemper:** a highly contagious respiratory disease that is often fatal in puppies.

• **Infectious Canine Hepatitis (ICH):** also a highly contagious virus, ICH is a potentially fatal disease that causes fever, eye and nose discharge, hemorrhaging, and lesions in the liver, kidney, and spleen.

• **Canine Parvovirus (CPV):** often fatal viral infection that causes severe vomiting and diarrhea.

• **Rabies:** a deadly virus affecting the nervous system that is transmitted when infected saliva comes in contact with an open cut or sore, or a dog's eyes, nose, or mouth.

Follow-up Protocol for Core Vaccinations

After a puppy receives his initial series of vaccinations, the current recommendation is for healthy adult Boxers to receive "booster" vaccinations for distemper, parvovirus, and canine hepatitis every three years. The rabies vaccination is slightly different in that it is given once (when the puppy is four months old), and is followed up 12 months later with an "adult" dose of the vaccine. How often rabies boosters are administered after the Boxer's first adult dose will be either annually or every three years, depending on regulations that are set by individual municipalities or states.

Noncore Vaccinations

Noncore vaccinations are considered to be optional; whether a particular noncore vaccine will be of benefit to your Boxer will require you and your veterinarian to carefully weigh the risks and benefits of each particular vaccine, with your Boxer's age, opportunity for exposure, and overall health.

Parasites: In and Out

Good veterinary care can prevent and treat infestations of the most common parasites affecting the Boxer. Prevention is always preferable to eradication of parasites. By preventing parasites from making a meal of your Boxer, not only are you limiting the possibility for transmission of disease from the parasites, but you are also preventing serious health problems (death included) from the infestation of a particular parasite.

Common parasites include: intestinal worms, heartworm, protozoa, fleas, and ticks.

Noncore Vaccinations

Disease	Virus or Bacteria	Dogs at Greatest Risk
Parainfluenza	A viral respiratory infection often present with *Bordatella*	Puppies and dogs with high exposure to other canines, such as those that are boarded at kennels, taken to dog shows, or frequently attend play groups or dog parks
Bordatella	Bacterial, also known as kennel cough or tracheobronchitis	Same as above
Lyme Disease	A bacteria spread by ticks, most commonly the deer tick	Dogs that live or travel to woody areas in the Northeast and upper Midwest, and parts of the West where deer ticks harboring the disease are most likely to be present
Leptospirosis	Bacterium that damages a dog's internal organs, in particular the kidneys and liver, and is spread through infected livestock and wildlife	Dogs that live, work, or play in areas with water supplies that come in contact with livestock and wildlife; highest risks are during summer and fall, and/or in temperate climates
Rattlesnake Bite Venom	The toxic components of snake venom cause tissue damage, organ failure, and disrupted blood clotting	Boxers that live in or travel to areas where rattlesnakes are present; search and rescue dogs; this vaccine may prevent serious or fatal reactions to snakebites from several different types of snakes
Canine Periodontitis	Multiple bacteria in the mouth that are suspected in causing tooth decay and gum disease	The Boxer's crowded premolars increase the risk of early onset of periodontal disease. The efficacy of this vaccine is still being proven; however, it is something that Boxer owners should be aware of and consider if results are positive

Parasites

Parasite	Symptoms	Diagnosis	Treatment	Prevention
Hookworms, whipworms, tapeworms, roundworms	In severe infections: anemia, distended belly, lusterless coat, weight loss, and vomiting or diarrhea	Fecal exam	Worming medications	Broad spectrum heartworm preventives also protect from infestations of many intestinal worms
Protozoa: *Giardia, Coccidia*	Diarrhea, which may or may not contain blood, usually thin, watery, and mucosal; vomiting (more common with *giardia*), weight loss, and overall poor condition	Fecal exam	Limiting reproduction of protozoa with antibiotics; Metronidazole for *giardia;* Sulfadimethoxine for *Coccidia*	Prevent exposure to contaminated water, feces
Heartworm	A cough is often the first symptom; advanced cases may include listlessness and weight loss.	Blood test	Arsenic-based drugs administered in a veterinary hosptial	Monthly oral or topical prescription preventives
Fleas	Itching, flea biting; flea dirt (when wet, leaves a bloody spot); red pin-prick-sized bites; presence of fleas	Presence of fleas	Flea shampoos, dips, powders; flea combs; treatment of all bedding (wash in sanitary cycle); vacuum all surfaces; repeat weekly for six to eight weeks; treat lawn if necessary	Monthly, topical flea preventive; also some oral varieties for non-breeding dogs
Ticks	Ticks on dog; Lyme disease; ehrlichiosis, canine anaplasmosis; and Rocky Mountain Spotted Fever	Tick-borne illnesses are diagnosed through blood tests	Antibiotics	Oral or topical flea and tick preventives

Diseases and Conditions of the Boxer

The following "top 10" diseases are grouped according to when a Boxer puppy or dog is most likely to begin showing symptoms of these diseases; however, it is possible for symptoms to appear sooner or later than as grouped below.

Puppies to One Year

Boxer ARVC: Boxer Arrhythmogenic Right Ventricular Cardiomyopathy (ARVC), formerly known as "Boxer Cardiomyopathy," is the leading cause of sudden death in Boxers. Boxer ARVC causes the heart to contract prematurely, creating an inefficient heartbeat. Prolonged sequences of premature beats can cause heart failure. As of May 2009, a genetic test is available to determine if a dog has the disease, is a carrier, or is free of ARVC. Breeders who use this test will be able to make ARVC a disease of the past in their lines.

There is no cure; however, current treatment for Boxers with ARVC include antiarrhythmic therapy, combined with diuretics and Angiotensin Converting Enzyme (ACE) inhibitors.

Subaortic stenosis (SAS): This heart disease, which produces an audible heart murmur, usually develops by the time the puppy is four to six months old. Basically, the disease causes a thickening of the area directly below the aortic valve, which is responsible for pumping oxygen-rich blood from the heart into the body through the aorta. As the subaortic area thickens, it prevents efficient passage of blood. The heart must pump harder to force blood through the narrowed valve, causing a turbulent sound, or murmur.

Currently, no cure is known for this disease; however, beta-blockers are used to prevent the affected heart from racing, which in turn could cause syncope or heart failure.

Hip dysplasia: Hip dysplasia is the top cause of hind leg lameness in dogs, including the Boxer. Though not nearly as common in the Boxer as it is with many of the larger, heavier breeds, hip dysplasia can cause severely arthritic hips in a much younger dog. The disease begins with an ill-fitting femur and hip socket: the hip socket may be too shallow and the ball of the femur does not fit tightly. A loose joint allows for excess movement, tiny fractures that heal roughly, creating a worse fit, and a vicious cycle of fracturing, healing, destruction of cushioning cartilage, and increasingly irregular fitting joints.

Boxers with severe hip dysplasia may require surgery. Boxers with less advanced disease may find relief with joint supplements, antiinflammatories, and pain medications. Keeping a Boxer at an ideal weight and fit through gentle exercise may also help to slow the progression of this condition.

TIP

Hip Dysplasia

Hip dysplasia is believed to have a genetic factor, and for this reason before a Boxer is bred, the breeder should have the dog's hips certified to be clear of disease, from either the Orthopedic Foundation for Animals (OFA) or the University of Pennsylvania Hip Improvement Program (PennHip).

Adult Boxers

Allergies: Boxers seem to be prone to allergies, both environmental (dust mites, pollen, grasses, mold, etc.) and food-related. Regardless of the source of the allergy, Boxers typically respond to allergens with an itchy, scaly skin that can become infected, and/or ear infections.

In order to treat the symptoms, the source of the allergy needs to be determined, and changes made to the Boxer's environment where possible, and/or the Boxer's food. With serious allergies, your veterinarian will most likely refer you and your dog to a specialist for more definitive testing or a food trial (if a food allergy is suspected), and the development of a treatment program.

Bloat: Roughly 50,000 dogs suffer from gastric dilatation-volvulus (GDV), or "bloat," each year and nearly 30 percent do not survive. GDV causes a twisting of the stomach that cuts off the blood supply to and from the stomach. If not treated immediately, the dog will die.

GDV primarily affects large and extra-large dog breeds, with the Boxer one of those breeds that appears to be predisposed. Despite years of research, the causes of bloat and its prevention are still largely unknown but individual studies have given Boxer owners some helpful insights:

✔ In a 1997 study, factors that were seen to *increase* a dog's risk for GDV included male gender, underweight, fed one meal a day, rapid eating of the meal, and a fearful temperament. Qualities that were cited as *decreasing* the risk of GDV were a "happy" temperament and the inclusion of table foods in a diet that consisted primarily of dry dog food. Additionally, the only factor that precipitated an acute episode of GDV was stress.

✔ In 2000, a study found that "the only breed-specific characteristic significantly associated

━━━CHECKLIST━━━

Know the Signs of Bloat
- A distended, swollen belly
- Unproductive attempts to vomit
- Shortness of breath
- Restlessness
- Anxiety
- Panting
- Whining
- Collapse

with a decreased incidence of GDV was an owner-perceived personality trait of happiness."

✔ A 2004 study confirmed that one large single meal increased a dog's risk for GDV, as did feeding a dog a meal with a high volume of food, regardless of the number of meals fed per day.

✔ In a 2006 study, dry food containing an oil or fat ingredient (sunflower oil, animal fat) among the first four ingredients was associated with a 2.4-fold increased risk of GDV.

✔ And in 2007, the risk of GDV was found to be negatively associated with the daily maximum temperature but extreme changes in barometric pressure or large drops in temperature were not predictive of disease.

So, your best bet at this time is to make sure your Boxer is as stress-free as possible, that he doesn't gulp down his food (placing toys in the bowl and making him eat around his food can help slow down eating), feeding him several small meals during the day (as opposed to one large meal), and making sure you know the early symptoms of bloat, so if something *does*

happen, you don't delay in getting your Boxer emergency veterinary care.

Cancer: Unfortunately, a disproportionate number of Boxers are afflicted with cancer, making this breed one of the top sufferers of many types of cancer, including: brain tumors, hemangiosarcoma (a tumor involving blood vessels), lymphosarcoma/lymphoma (a cancer of a specific type of blood cell), osteosarcoma (bone cancer), and mast cell tumors (a common form of skin cancer).

Depending on the type of cancer and its location, some cancers can be cured, others may be slowed in their progression, while the most aggressive of cancers may have a much more limited prognosis. Treatment options may include surgery, chemotherapy, radiation, cryosurgery (freezing), hyperthermia (heating), or immunotherapy. Pain management is an important part of any cancer treatment program, too. The goal of all treatment programs is to provide the Boxer with a longer, higher quality life than would be possible without treatment.

With cancer, an early diagnosis is crucial to the prognosis, treatment plan, quality of life, and potential outcome for your Boxer. All Boxer owners should be aware of the following ten early indicators of cancer as provided by the American Veterinary Medical Association (AVMA):

✔ Abnormal swellings that persist or continue to grow
✔ Sores that do not heal
✔ Weight loss
✔ Loss of appetite
✔ Bleeding or discharge from any body opening
✔ Offensive odor
✔ Difficulty eating or swallowing
✔ Hesitation to exercise or loss of stamina
✔ Persistent lameness or stiffness
✔ Difficulty breathing, urinating, or defecation

Corneal Epithelial Erosion: This painful condition is not so much a disease as it is a result of the anatomy of the Boxer's eye. Breeds that have larger, protruding eyes (particularly brachycephalic breeds) have a higher incidence of damage to the cornea. The damage may be a one-time trauma, or it may be repetitive in nature, such as the continued scratching of the cornea by eyelashes.

Usually, if the injury is slight, the cornea will heal itself. If the injury is more severe, the cornea could develop an ulcer that deepens

further into the eye, potentially causing blindness and great pain.

If you notice your Boxer squinting in the sun, blinking a bit too much, rubbing his eyes, tearing, or showing signs of pain, seek veterinary care immediately. Treatment may include topical antibiotics, such as eyedrops, as well as other medications to reduce pain and supplement tear production.

Degenerative Myelopathy (DM): DM is a hereditary disease that is similar to multiple sclerosis in people. Over the course of many years, DM slowly destroys the messaging system from the brain to the muscles, rendering the muscles incapable of carrying out the movement messages being sent to them by the brain.

The first signs of DM are toe dragging or knuckling over of the back paws. As the disease progresses, the Boxer loses more control in his rear legs until his hind end becomes completely paralyzed.

There is no cure for DM; however, there are several things owners can do to make their Boxers more comfortable and potentially slow the progression of the disease. Exercise, particularly swimming and gentle walking in the early stages of the disease, can increase muscle tone and allow the dog to move with less stress on the joints. Also, keeping your Boxer at an appropriate weight will keep stress on his joints to a minimum. Dog booties on the rear paws will lessen damage to his nails and knuckles. And, make sure your Boxer has secure footing throughout the house (i.e., carpets, nonslip mats, etc.).

TIP

Test

There is now a genetic test for degenerative myelopathy, which allows breeders to know if their dogs have the disease, carry the disease, or are genetically clear of the disease. This will allow breeders who test their dogs to ensure that no future generations of puppies suffer from DM.

Demodectic Mange: More research is required in this area; however, Boxers—particularly those under stress—appear to be more susceptible to skin disorders that are linked with immune mediated disease. In particular, many Boxers suffer from severe cases of demodectic mange.

Demodex mites naturally inhabit hair follicles and oil glands in a healthy dog's skin. For whatever reason, as soon as a dog's immune system is compromised, the number of mites in the hair follicles explodes. "Red Mange" as it is sometimes called, may start with the dry form (in which there is hair loss and redness of the skin), which can quickly develop into a much more serious condition with secondary bacterial infections that can be fatal.

Treatment involves veterinary care that may include prescription shampoos, dips, antibiotics, and an injectible wormer, among other medications. Until the Boxer regains a strong immune system, however, the mites can continue to be a chronic problem.

Hypothyroidism: This condition is common in all breeds of dogs, but Boxers appear to be genetically predisposed to hypothyroidism. Over a period of months or years, the dog's immune system forms antibodies that attack the thyroid gland, resulting in the complete (or near complete) destruction of the thyroid *and* the thyroid's ability to produce hormones.

Symptoms of hypothyroidism include lethargy, hair loss, obesity, dry hair coat, and skin problems. The good news is that, once diagnosed, hypothyroidism is generally simple to treat with a daily dose of a synthetic thyroid hormone for the life of the dog. Once on the correct dosage, most, if not all, of the dog's symptoms usually disappear.

Prompt Veterinary Care

The bottom line with Boxers is that if you see a change, either behaviorally or physically, seek veterinary attention immediately. Boxers are masters at being martyrs and not showing signs or symptoms of pain until a disease or condition is quite advanced. To detect a disease early on, Boxer owners need to be adept at picking up subtle changes in their dog. As the person who knows your Boxer better than anyone else, you will pick up on changes before you might understand what you are seeing.

UNDERSTANDING YOUR BOXER

Understanding how your Boxer sees her world can help you recognize why she behaves the way she does, and then channel her positive attributes to develop a well-behaved, social pet.

How a Boxer Sees the World

The Boxer was selectively bred to have exceptional scenting abilities, keen hearing, and good vision. With such sharp senses, the Boxer was developed to be alert to even the most subtle changes in her environment.

So, what does this mean to you? The Boxer will not miss anything.

Scenting Abilities

The Boxer is able to detect scents that have been diluted to just a few parts per million. Therefore, finding the most minuscule crumb that has fallen between the stove and a cabinet is simple for the Boxer.

The Boxer's incredible sense of smell also enables her to pick up on subtle changes in your emotions. This is in part due to the Boxer's ability to smell the emission of hormones.

Though we (humans) can't "smell fear" or aggression, the Boxer *can*. For owners who are timid, this perceptive ability of the Boxer is something to consider. If you are apprehensive or nervous while walking your Boxer, your Boxer will *instinctively* look for a reason for your fears. This can result in a dog that is overly protective, which will often increase a timid owner's apprehensions, creating a vicious cycle that creates an increasingly reactive Boxer.

Hearing

The Boxer has very sharp hearing. Whether her ears are cropped or natural, she will hear *everything*. Just try to say the word "cookie" or open a snack package without your Boxer running to your side, in hopes of a tasty morsel. This finely tuned sense of hearing also means that your Boxer will not miss a sound in or out of your home. The Boxer is not only an excellent watchdog, but also an outstanding "filter" for

those who live alone. The well-adjusted Boxer won't alert you to the normal creaks and pops of an older home; she will only alert you to unusual sounds—those that need your attention.

Vision

Though not possessing the long-distance acuity of a sighthound, the Boxer is particularly adept at detecting movement in the near to middle distance range. This motion-detecting vision functions not only in bright daylight, but in fading light as well. At dusk, when we might miss a movement in the brush, for example, the Boxer will see it.

The Sum of the Parts

The Boxer's incredible sense of smell, hearing, and sight means that as a pet, the Boxer is not going to miss *anything* in the home or out. Virtually any changes in her environment are going to be noted. How she reacts to changes in her world depends largely on her inherited temperament, and her life experiences. You cannot control her genetic makeup; however, you *can* control the quality of your Boxer's experiences. The place in which you can make a particularly positive impact is with your Boxer's friendliness toward people.

Socialization with People

The Boxer is, by nature, a confident, outgoing breed. A well-bred Boxer will want to meet people and will greet friendly strangers with the trademark, Boxer wriggle—the nubbin' wag that starts at the dog's docked tail and continues up through her body until her entire body is doing a big body wag. The friendliness of this wriggle is unmistakable.

Unfortunately, not all Boxers are born to have the "classic" Boxer temperament. Two types of temperaments that are difficult to overcome are the timid dog, and the reactive/mistrustful dog.

With timid Boxers, fear biting can become an issue. Fear biting occurs when a dog is afraid of an individual and feels she has no way to escape the person. Fear biting is the number one cause of dog bites. For this reason, it is critically important that owners of timid Boxers work to *safely* build their dogs' confidence with people.

The other temperament, which was previously unheard of in the Boxer, is the highly reactive dog. These Boxers are not shy. They are bold and pushy and can be quick to react to what they perceive as a challenge or a threat. Often a trigger for aggressive behavior can be as minor as a stranger making glancing eye contact with the Boxer. The reactive Boxer is a difficult dog for an experienced handler—much less a novice owner—to handle. If your Boxer appears to have aggressive tendencies toward people, it is important to seek out a professional trainer, preferably someone who is experienced with Boxers, in particular.

Making Socialization Successful

With the understanding that not every Boxer is born with the perfect temperament, it is important that you help your Boxer reach her full potential as a people-friendly dog. Of primary importance is that your Boxer associates only good things with people.

No bad experiences: When it comes to socialization with people, it's not the quantity of people you introduce your Boxer to that will make her a social butterfly; rather, it's the quality of the meetings. If possible, every person your Boxer meets should lead to a pleasant, positive experience. In order for this to happen, you have to recognize when your Boxer is comfortable and when she's not. Meet and greets can go forward only if your puppy or adult dog is completely relaxed and comfortable.

Know your Boxer's friendly body language: A Boxer that is comfortable and happy is fairly easy to read. She will have a loose, relaxed body; her docked tail will be wagging gently in mid-height position; if she's very happy and a bit excited, she will be in a full body wiggle; her ears will be in a relaxed position or in a "soft" prick; and she will have a big, wide-mouthed pant (if she's warm). Her overall demeanor is happy and relaxed.

Recognize key signs of stress: Stressed dogs usually behave in one of several ways; the dog could become aggressive, fearful, or what

appears to be "frantically friendly." If she is taking an aggressive stance, she will appear to stiffen as her body muscles tighten and bulge; she may stand more erectly on her toes; her eyes may narrow; pupils enlarge; her tail may be erect and wagging stiffly; and she may begin to growl or bark. If she is frightened, she may visibly shrink her body stance or cower; she may shake or tremble; her tail will curl tightly between her legs; she may try to hide behind you or run away; and if pushed, she may switch into an aggressive posture in a last-ditch effort to get the approaching person to go away. Another response that is commonly misinterpreted as being a positive behavior is the "frantically" friendly puppy or dog. This dog is not relaxed but truly appears frantic—jumping up, cowering, spinning around—in her confused, mixed greet-

ing of strangers. This, too, is a highly stressed dog and the ensuing greeting with the stranger will not leave a positive impression on her.

Know the moment of transition: Of course, by the time the Boxer is showing clear signs of stress, the experience has already deteriorated. To keep all contacts with people positive, you must be able to stop the meeting *before she becomes stressed.* It sounds complicated but it's really quite easy: the *moment* your Boxer does not show friendly, relaxed body language, she is uneasy. *Move her farther away from the person she is meeting until she resumes her comfortable, relaxed body language.*

A Boxer's transition period may last only a second or two before she transitions into a state of stress, fear, or aggression, so you must be aware of what your Boxer is doing. Once your

Boxer is showing comfortable, relaxed body language, you can move forward with the meeting.

The following are some additional guidelines for socializing your Boxer with people:

✔ **Allow your Boxer to make her own approach:** Most confident, friendly Boxers have no problems walking up to strangers and receiving gentle strokes under the chin. If you don't have a confident Boxer, it is most important that you allow her—not the stranger—to make the approach.

✔ **Control how people greet your boxer:** Reaching over a dog's head (to pat her) can be scary to many dogs, particularly those who are wary about being "collared" (grabbed by the collar). A much better approach is to have strangers offer an open hand, palm up to the Boxer, and scratch the dog under her chin or on the cheek. Particularly timid dogs will appreciate no attempts to pet them; here the goal (and reward) is for the Boxer to touch the person's hand. Other human behaviors that a less confident Boxer may find intimidating, and ones that you should make sure that strangers do not do to your Boxer, include direct eye contact (have greeters avoid looking directly into the eyes of a timid Boxer); bending over the dog to pet it; putting their faces in the Boxer's face; and, with children, crowding around the Boxer with lots of clamoring and noise.

✔ **Reward good behavior and touches:** When your Boxer greets a stranger with confidence and friendliness, often the verbal and physical praise from the stranger is rewarding in itself. If you are working with a less confident dog, however, pats may not be a reward. Instead, have strangers offer your Boxer treats. This achieves three things: (1) the dog receives an instant reward for coming up to the stranger; (2) the

A Special Word on Aggression

A common complaint of readers is:

Why can't you tell me how to work with my aggressive Boxer? There are several reasons for this. First, there is no way to describe in a few pages the myriad of subtle body language clues that a dog may exhibit prior to an act of aggression—the clues *you* need to be able to prevent bad Boxer behavior or a serious bite. Additionally, aggressive behavior cannot be curbed until it can be determined what type or types of aggression the Boxer is exhibiting. There are believed to be dozens of kinds of aggression; most dogs display more than one form. Depending on the form of aggression, the Boxer will react to different "triggers," or types of things that trigger the Boxer to behave aggressively. The only way to determine the types and cause of the Boxer's aggressive behavior is for an experienced trainer or behaviorist to observe and work with the dog and owner. Then, a positive, reward-based training program can be tailored to the dog's needs, and hopefully, working with the trainer, much progress can be made in getting to the heart of the problem and coming up with workable solutions.

Boxer is allowed to make her own approach; and (3) it prevents the stranger from making many of the potentially dominant moves that we humans often make unintentionally.

✔ **Consider clicker training:** A great way to work with socialization is by clicker training. With clicker training, the Boxer first is taught to associate the sound of the click with a treat. Once this is established, a click can be given to the Boxer to let her know she did something

correctly and a treat is coming. The clicker can be used to shape a behavior, such as touching a stranger on the fingertips when he or she extends a hand. One of the advantages to clicker training is that the handler can pinpoint the desired behavior with a click, which cuts down on confusion for the dog. (For more information on clicker training, see Resources, page 93.)

Socialization with Dogs

Much of the body language between dogs is universal. Your Boxer is born with the innate ability to understand other dogs' intentions, as well as express her intentions to other dogs.

While playing with littermates, puppies put their instincts into practice, honing their skills in communicating with other dogs. They learn when a bite is too hard (bite inhibition), how to initiate play, when play is too rough, and the body language of "Enough," which is usually taught by the puppy's mother.

Boxers that continue to socialize with friendly dogs after they've left the breeder's home are often very comfortable playing with all types of dogs. Dogs that don't continue to play with other dogs, or those that are separated from their littermates at an early age (prior to seven weeks of age), may be awkward in their greeting and play behaviors. Practice truly does make for better, more easily interpreted intentions.

You can build on this foundation by allowing your Boxer to play with friendly, social puppies

---

TIP

Playing Well With Others

Some Boxers, when they reach maturity, do not play well with others no matter how well socialized they were as young dogs. A social Boxer is great, but keep in mind that if your Boxer isn't dog-friendly, it's not the end of the world. If she is terrific with people, and polite when on-leash (around other dogs), you have a wonderful companion.

and dogs. Puppy owners need to be cautious, however, where they take their puppies and with whom they play, since puppies are not fully vaccinated (and protected from disease) until they are nearly four months old.

The best way to socialize your Boxer is to keep all play sessions positive. One frightening experience can make a permanent impression on a young dog, which she may or may not overcome as an adult dog.

The following are some tips for keeping play sessions fun for your Boxer:

✔ Select friendly, vaccinated, healthy dogs.

✔ Keep it equal. Puppies should not play with dogs that are more than twice their size; adult dogs should not play with very small dogs (just because of the size difference and the potential for injury).

✔ Watch for changes in body language. In particular, look for signs that a puppy is becoming stressed or frightened, and an adult dog is becoming aggressive or bullying.

✔ Make the dogs take timeouts. To prevent hard play from escalating into a squabble, call your Boxer out of the play group every so often and have her lie down for several minutes (a "cool down" period) before rejoining the group.

✔ Keep groups small. Some dogs are comfortable playing with one or maybe two dogs; others can play in much larger groups. Adjust the size of the group according to your Boxer's comfort level.

✔ Play off leash. If you're not sure how your Boxer is going to react to the other dogs in a play group, allow your dog to drag her leash. *Do not hold her leash.* Many dogs display aggressive behaviors when on-leash because they feel trapped or limited in their movements.

✔ Go with your gut instincts. If you feel play is about to go over the top, or if you think your Boxer is not enjoying herself, remove her from the group. You are the best judge as to your Boxer's comfort level, and it's always better to be too safe than to be sorry later.

BASIC TRAINING

Training your Boxer not only provides you with a way to keep him mentally and physically stimulated (and out of trouble), it also enables you to establish and maintain leadership in a nonconfrontational manner.

Principles of Positive, Reward-based Training

Boxers learn behaviors in one of two ways—either in a positive manner or in a negative manner. With positive, reward-based training, when the Boxer offers the correct behavior, he is rewarded with praise, play, a treat, etc. He quickly learns to provide the desired behavior in order to receive his reward. Positive training also enables the handler to use lures to position the dog. It's a hands-free method of training that allows even sensitive and reactive dogs to be trained in a nonconfrontational way.

With negative reinforcement training, the Boxer is punished if he does not provide the correct behavior. The punishment may be a pop on a training collar or a more severe physical correction. Through this manner of training, he learns to provide the correct behavior in order to avoid discomfort or pain.

Both methods of training work, and sometimes the methods are combined; however, positive, reward-based training is much more fun for both Boxer and owner, *and* this method of training generally produces a much more eager learner and overall happier Boxer.

Timing

When teaching a dog a new behavior, the timing of the verbal command is important. If you say the command, "*Sit*" before the dog is sitting, he may learn to squat or continue standing for the *sit* command. If you repeat the command multiple times before the dog finally sits, he will learn to wait until you've said the command multiple times before he gives you the desired behavior.

The *Right* Time

When training a new behavior, the verbal command should be given *as the Boxer gives the desired behavior.* When training a *sit*, for example, you should use a food or toy lure to position your Boxer into a *sit* (more on this in a moment). As he sits squarely on the floor—when there is no possible chance he will not sit—say, "*Sit.*" Then give him the reward, which is the food lure, or a chance to play with a toy (if you've used a toy as a lure), and always, verbal praise (Good boy!) and physical praise (pats and rubs). As he learns a behavior, you can gradually eliminate the lure and give the verbal command sooner. You will know when your Boxer is really "getting it," because he will perform the behavior quickly and with confidence.

Teaching the Basics: *Sit, Down, Come, Walk Nicely*

There are many different ways to teach the basic commands of *sit, down,* and *come.* And, there are even more ways to teach a puppy or adult dog to *walk nicely* on a leash. The following are some very basic guidelines for teaching these skills; however, as you work with your Boxer, you may find it's easier to use a different technique. That's fine!

The importance of positive, reward-based training is that you, as your Boxer's trainer, are able to keep the training sessions positive, *fun* (the Boxer should never realize he's being trained). With puppies, multiple sessions that last only a few minutes sprinkled throughout the day can be a very successful way of getting in many repetitions of a skill in one day without boring the Boxer. Older dogs with longer attention spans can work longer sessions; however, short training periods throughout the day to teach basic obedience skills works for any age dog.

Teaching the *Sit*

Puppies as young as five and six weeks old are capable of learning the *sit* command. In fact, you might find that your eight-week-old puppy comes to you already trained to this command. If this is not the case, or if you've adopted an adult Boxer with little or no training, don't fret—Boxers of any age are capable of learning this command very, very quickly.

Luring

In order to teach a dog to *sit* on command, the dog must associate the action of sitting with the word, "*Sit.*" And, in order to link the action of sitting with the word, "*Sit,*" the Boxer will need to sit many times while hearing the word, "*Sit.*" For this to happen, you must have a reliable way to get your Boxer to sit, any time and every time you want this behavior. One of the easiest ways to do this is to use a treat as a lure.

Holding the Boxer gently by the collar in one hand (to prevent him from sidestepping or backing up), and with a tiny food treat in the other, slowly move the treat from the tip of the Boxer's nose, between his eyes and backward toward the space between his ears. Your hand should be close enough to the Boxer's head that you nearly brush your fingers against him.

As you move the treat *slowly* over his head, your Boxer should fold backward into a sitting position. At first, it may take a little while for your Boxer to figure out this is what you want. He may squat, or he may try to back up to get the treat. That's okay—he will figure it out!

Wait For It . . .

The *moment* your Boxer plants himself into a solid *sit*, say *"Sit!"* Reward him with the treat, give him lots of praise, and release him from the *sit*, with a release command, such as *"Okay!"* Then repeat the exercise. Try to work in multiple repetitions throughout the day. Your goal is to have your Boxer easily following the lure and folding eagerly into a *sit* for at least eight out of the last ten repetitions before you make the exercise a little harder.

Step two is to give the command a little earlier in the *sit*, so that the Boxer connects the word, *"Sit"* with the act of sitting. As you move the treat and your Boxer begins to fold into a *sit*, say *"Sit"* at the point at which you are 99 percent certain that your Boxer will complete his sit. If he appears unsteady or uncertain as to what you want (he is sitting very slowly, for example), use the lure to shape the *sit* and return to saying, *"Sit"* as he finishes the *sit*. After eight out of ten correct repetitions (and these can be spread out during the day), try to give your Boxer the *sit* command when he's about halfway into his *sit*. After eight of ten successful repetitions, try giving the command at the beginning of the *sit*.

Phasing Out Treats

At the beginning of this exercise, you will be giving your Boxer a treat after every successful repetition. He's learning a new skill and the

treats are used not only to shape the behavior (sitting) but also to reinforce that he has performed the *sit* correctly. When you've got your Boxer to the point at which you can say *"Sit!"* and he will slam down into a *sit*, you can be more random in rewarding with treats. (You'll still reward him with praise, however.)

Teaching the *Down*

The *down* is a little trickier to teach than the *sit*. Using a lure/treat makes shaping the *down*

goal is to get your Boxer to follow the treat to the floor without raising his rear end. If he moves down a little, you can give him the treat and tell him he's a good boy. Next time, he has to move a little farther down to the floor before he gets the treat and praise. Continue working to get him lower and lower until he finally is lying down. Say, "*Down*!" give him the treat, and praise him.

Repetition

Continue to lure your Boxer into the *down* until he is going down quickly and steadily. Continue to link the command, "*Down*!" with the position of lying down. Continue luring him into the *down*, and start to give the command, "*Down*!" a little sooner each time. Eventually, you'll be able to say the command without using the lure.

Practice, practice, practice. Make training fun for your Boxer and keep up his enthusiasm. If the *down* is something that is hard for your Boxer, be sure to finish your training session with a command or trick that he has learned that he thinks is fun and that he knows very well. This will boost his confidence and helps to keep up his enthusiasm for learning new skills.

easier; however, many dogs have trouble following the lure to the floor without their rear ends popping up in back. Since luring a Boxer into a full, complete *down* may be more difficult, you can work on the *down* in smaller segments, rewarding your dog for making progress. The key to this method is that you don't say the word, "*Down*," until your Boxer is actually lying down.

Luring

Put your Boxer in a *sit*. Then, holding his collar gently to steady him, take a treat and slowly move it slightly forward and to the floor. Your

Teaching Your Boxer to *Come*

Perhaps the most valuable command you might ever teach your Boxer is the *come* command. If taught properly, your Boxer should wheel around and come running to you every time you call him. The problem is that many owners don't work on this command *or* they don't teach it quite right.

The principle to teaching this command is actually quite simple: ensure that your Boxer virtually can't fail.

Ensuring Perfection

In order to set your Boxer up to succeed with the *recall*, or *come* command, you need to set up situations in which you are absolutely sure that your Boxer will come to you. And then, you must use these opportunities to link the command, "*Come!*" with the action of coming. Here are some ways to work on this important command.

Off leash:

✔ When your puppy is running toward you in the hallway of your home, say "*Come!*" Praise him for being such a good boy and give him treats.

✔ Have family members hide in areas of the house loaded with yummy doggie treats. Take turns saying, "*Puppy, puppy, puppy!*" to let him know where you are. When he comes running for you, say "*Come!*"

✔ In a fenced-in area (such as your backyard), get your Boxer to run toward you *by running away from him.* Turn around to face him, and if he is running toward you, say "*Come!*"

✔ Take advantage of any off-leash opportunity to use the command, "*Come!*" but only when you are 99 percent sure that your Boxer is coming to you. For example, when you are getting your Boxer's dinner, and he comes running over to you, say "Come!" If you go to get his leash for his morning walk and he comes running to have you snap it to his collar, say "*Come!*

On leash:

When your Boxer is on leash, there are multiple opportunities for you to work on the *come* command.

✔ While walking your dog, start walking backward. When your Boxer realizes you are going the opposite direction, encourage him to turn and trot or gallop toward you. As soon as he

has changed direction and is happily coming toward you, say "*Come!*"

✔ Your goal, whether inside or outside the home, on or off leash, is to maximize the number of times you can link the command for *come* with your Boxer actually coming to you—and preferably at a high rate of speed. Practice, practice, practice. And always keep it fun!

So, what do you do if you need to call your Boxer and you're not sure he'll come to you? If it's an emergency and he is in danger of being seriously injured or killed, call him in as pleasant and happy a tone as possible. Use the command if you've been working with him on it. If he doesn't respond to you, try moving away

from him in the opposite direction. Most dogs will turn and follow you. Whatever you do, try not to become angry or agitated with him. This will result in a game of keep-away, and Boxers are masters of the art of dodging and keeping just out of hand's reach.

Once you've got him back safely, resolve to work on the *come* command on a regular basis, as often as possible.

Walking Nicely

Depending on whether you've purchased a puppy or adopted an adult Boxer, your issues of walking your Boxer may be completely

different. Typically, the young puppy *wants* to follow you but isn't sure about the whole idea of being tied to a leash. The adult dog has no problems with being on leash; here the issue is who is walking whom. Both problems are easily solved.

Puppy Walking

When you clip your puppy to the leash, he will want to chew and play with it. Gently encourage him to follow you *but don't pull him*. Puppies react to pressure in the same way that horses do: if you pull, they will pull back. That's not what you want; you want the puppy to follow you. To do this, talk to him, give him treats when he puts his nose to your hand while you're walking, and be careful to get his attention when he's distracted, rather than pulling him.

Small puppies cannot go for long walks; once around the block may be enough for an eight-week-old puppy. But, be sure to work on walking your young puppy and encouraging him to stay with you. This will prevent the Boxer from getting into the habit of pulling. Which brings us to our next age group...

Adult Boxers

Older puppies that have never been taught to walk on a leash at an early age and adult dogs that have been neglected and never walked, will often have the same problem—they pull. There are many ways to work on *walking nicely*. Here are just a few.

✔ **Treat him:** Wear a hip pack filled with a portion of your Boxer's dinner. At suppertime, take him for a walk and constantly feed him little bits of his dinner to keep his attention and keep him close to you.

✔ **Directional challenge:** When on a walk, constantly change directions to encourage your Boxer to pay attention to you. It may look a bit crazy (and the neighbors may question your sanity) but the principle is this: whatever direction your Boxer wants to forge ahead in, you take the opposite direction. When the Boxer changes direction and catches up to you, praise him. Give him treats.

✔ **Consider training aids:** If your Boxer is not interested in treats, and is so strong and so pushy on walks that you can't control him by changing directions, consider using a head halter or a no-pull harness. These training aids are not cruel and effectively allow even the smallest owner to control even the strongest, most untrained Boxer. It is important to prop-

erly fit the Boxer to the devices, so be sure to consult with an experienced person. Because the Boxer is brachycephalic, it can be harder to fit this breed with the head halter; however, there are specific products made for this breed. Look for them and see which works best for your Boxer.

Activities for the Boxer

The Boxer is an eager and capable competitor in virtually every sport and activity offered to dogs. The hardest decision you might have to make is not which sport in which you want to participate, but how many!

The following is a list of activities and sports with information on each to get you interested.

Boxer Activities

Activity	Type	What It Is
Agility	Competitive	High-speed fun. Handler directs Boxer through a course of obstacles, ranging from teeter-totters to tunnels, ramps, and jumps
Conformation	Competitive	Boxers compete against each other in the show ring to earn points toward a championship. Males and females must not be altered. Boxers are judged on conformation, movement, and style. They must adhere to breed standard and have a stellar temperament
Dock Jumping	Competitive	Boxers jump off a dock into water to retrieve a toy. Prizes are awarded for longest jump, highest jump, and longest retrieve
Flyball	Competitive	A team of four dogs (one at a time) race over a series of hurdles to a box that releases a ball, which the Boxer must catch and return over the hurdles
Musical Freestyle	Competitive	Boxer is trained to perform specific movements with his handler that are choreographed to music
Obedience	Competitive	The basics for training "manners" comes from the entry level of obedience. Handlers can participate to earn titles (three passing scores), or to win placements
Schutzhund	Competitive; may also compete as pass/fail in tracking	A three-part test of obedience, tracking, and protection work
Weight Pull	Competitive	Wearing specially fitted harnesses (and using high-tech sleds or carts), dogs compete in weight classes to see who can pull the most weight

Noncompetitive Activities

Canine Good Citizen Test	Noncompetitive	Pass/Fail test. Handlers and dogs are tested on basic skills that are important to well-behaved companions

Contact Information

American Kennel Club (AKC)
Canine Performance Events, Inc. (CPE)
North American Dog Agility Council (NADAC)
United Kennel Club (UKC)
United States Dog Agility Association (USDAA)

American Kennel Club (AKC)
United Kennel Club (UKC)

DockDogs
United Kennel Club (UKC)

North American Flyball Association (NAFA)

World Canine Freestyle Organization
Musical Dog Sport Association

American Kennel Club (AKC)
United Kennel Club (UKC)

DVG America
United States Boxer Association

American Pulling Alliance
International Weight Pull Association
Iron Dog International
United Kennel Club (UKC)

American Kennel Club (AKC)

Boxer Activities (continued)

Activity	Type	What It Is
Carting	Noncompetitive	Boxers pull specially balanced carts through a pattern with only the handler's commands
Rally	Noncompetitive	Set up with a different task/command to perform at each station, Rally allows the handler to talk to his or her Boxer through the entire test
Tracking	Noncompetitive	Pass/Fail for titles. Boxer tracks scent trails and finds articles left on varying terrain with different levels of difficulty
Search and Rescue (SAR)	Noncompetitive; service	Boxers have been amazing in SAR. It requires a physically fit owner, and a dog that is excellent at tracking. Searches are for live rescues or human remains
Animal-Assisted Therapy	Noncompetitive; service	Another amazing opportunity for the Boxer. Steady temperament required. Training and certification is completed through a national organization

Contact Information

Certifications are offered by a wide range of
working dog breed clubs, which, with space
available, allow all breeds to participate

American Kennel Club (AKC)
Association of Pet Dog Trainers (APDT)

American Kennel Club (AKC)

National Association for Search and Rescue, Inc.

The Delta Society
Therapy Dogs International, Inc.
R.E.A.D. (Reading Education Assistance Program)

SOLVING BEHAVIORAL PROBLEMS

Most of the behavior issues commonly seen in the Boxer can be prevented, and all can be modified or even eliminated with training.

Destructive Chewing

Boxers will chew for two reasons: teething and/or boredom.

Teething: At around four to five months, when the Boxer puppy is losing her milk teeth and her adult teeth are coming in, her gums are itchy, achy, and sore. She *needs* to chew to help rid her of dangling milk teeth and allow her erupting adult teeth to grow.

While a Boxer is teething, she will chew on anything. With substantial jaw power, this means that virtually anything in your home can be destroyed. To prevent massive destruction during this time, it is important to limit your Boxer's access to items she shouldn't be chewing (dog gates, exercise pens, and crates help during these months). It is equally important to give your Boxer safe items that she can chew 24/7. Hard rubber toys, such as Kongs, are ideal because they aren't so hard that a young Boxer will break a tooth; however, the larger sizes are durable enough that your Boxer won't be able to chew chunks off and choke on them.

Boredom: The second cause of destructive chewing, and the most common reason for an adult Boxer to tear up articles in the home, is boredom. A Boxer that is not given enough exercise and mental stimulation will turn to other activities. She will create her own excitement. To control this type of destructive chewing, make sure your Boxer is getting enough exercise. In addition, daily training will help to mentally stimulate your Boxer and keep her from seeking out inappropriate chew items. Also, limit the Boxer's access to items she shouldn't be eating. And, on a final note, if the Boxer is showing high levels of stress when you leave the home *and* then chewing pillows, drapes, windowsills, etc., it is very possible your Boxer is suffering from separation anxiety. (For more information on working with this issue see page 78.)

Excessive Barking

Boxers are terrific watchdogs but sometimes the act of barking at an approaching person can be self-rewarding. For example, the delivery man comes to the front door with a package. Your Boxer barks an alert. The delivery man drops the package and returns to his truck, the whole time your Boxer is barking. In your Boxer's mind, she has successfully driven the delivery man off with her barking. Her barking was rewarded (the man left) and she is more likely to repeat this behavior in the future.

The same self-rewarding process can occur when you accidentally reward her barking. Does your Boxer bark at you when she wants a treat? A walk? Attention? If you give her what she wants, *you* have just reinforced the behavior.

To control unnecessary barking, you can approach the problem from several different angles:

1. Remove the stimulus. If your Boxer barks at the front door, as noted previously, limit her access to the door when you can't be present. Crate her or put up dog gates to make the front door inaccessible.

2. Teach her to *hush/speak* on command. When your Boxer is barking, say, "*Speak!*" (You may also say "*Watch him!*" if you would like an element of protection from your Boxer's bark.) Reward her. *Then*, the moment she is quiet (and not just catching her breath), say, "*Hush!*" Reward her. Keep working on these commands and your Boxer will learn to bark and be quiet when you ask.

3. Teach the *down*. It's very difficult for a Boxer to bark when she is lying down. When your Boxer is barking at the front door, at you, or even on leash, put your Boxer in a *down*. Reward her for being quiet.

4. Exercise. A Boxer that is regularly taken outside of her home and into varying and new areas for vigorous exercise tends to be less overly protective of her property than the Boxer that remains cooped up inside a home all day.

Jumping Up

When a Boxer puppy jumps up to give you those amazing Boxer kisses, it's cute and adorable. When a full-grown Boxer jumps up eye level or bowls you over to give licks, it's

not so pleasant. The problem is that jumping up is a very friendly doggie greeting. The trick is to teach her some basic manners while not squashing the Boxer's enthusiasm for wanting to lavish love on people.

Teach the *sit*: Do not allow people to pet or treat your Boxer *unless she is sitting*. You will be amazed at how quickly your Boxer realizes that sitting will get her all the love and attention she craves.

Recognize when jumping up is not a friendly greeting: If a Boxer is not confident, she may display a kind of crazy, mixed-up greeting behavior. Often seen in puppies, the Boxer will seem to be overly excited to greet a person, and yet she also has the body language of a puppy that is highly stressed or fearful. These puppies *are* stressed and should be moved farther away from the stranger. When the puppy

shows signs of being relaxed and happy, *then* allow her to make a more controlled greeting.

On-Leash Aggression

A chief source of embarrassment among dog owners, and the reason why many Boxer owners stop walking their dogs completely, is on-leash aggression. Whenever another dog passes by, the Boxer barks and lunges and carries on. The good news is that very, very few Boxers are actually dog aggressive. And, the better news is that with a little work, you can regain control and quiet when on walks—with a little persistence, practice, and training.

Know your Boxer's "bubble": How far away from another dog does your Boxer need to be before she remains quiet? Ten feet? Twenty feet? On the other side of the street? Determine

what distance your Boxer needs to be from other dogs and create this distance for her.

Work to decrease this distance: Reward your Boxer when she displays relaxed, comfortable body language. Gradually work to reduce the distance from which you need to pass other dogs. Remember, the more good experiences she has (quiet, no barking, relaxed), the easier it will be to repeat this performance on your next outing.

Teach the *down*: As noted previously, it is nearly impossible for a Boxer that is in a *down* to bark.

Keep her busy: Take her mind off the approaching dog by quickening your pace (move from a walk into a jog), perform a series of fast-paced obedience exercises (*sit, down,*

sit, reverse directions, etc.), and reward her for good behavior and good completion of the exercises.

Maintain a loose leash. Often, owners anticipate their Boxer's lunging and barking and tighten up on the leash. This motion serves only to fuel the Boxer's poor behaviors, as the dog senses the owner's nervousness and anxiety. Instead, keep the leash slack. You want to have control but not send your Boxer the wrong message. If you keep to your "safe" distance (your Boxer's bubble), your Boxer *won't* lunge or bark, helping to keep both of you calm and relaxed.

Don't stop: Keep working with your Boxer. If you are diligent in helping her to be quiet around other dogs, she *will* improve.

Resource Guarding

When a Boxer growls or snarls to prevent other dogs or puppies from taking away a highly valued item (such as food, a chew bone, or a favorite toy), this is called "resource guarding."

Resource guarding becomes an issue when the Boxer guards an item from a family member. Initial warning signs may include tucking the item under the Boxer's chin as she lies almost on top of the item; growling; or snarling. A Boxer that is determined not to give up the item may increase her threats and lunge, snap, or bite the person reaching for the object. With forethought and some training, however, it is possible to work with a possessive Boxer to create a safer environment.

Teach the *give* command: Being able to ask a dog to give up even the most coveted item and know almost with certainty that the Boxer will release the item to you is an extremely valuable skill. To teach this command, you will need to teach the *take it* command at the same time. Take an item that your Boxer will find pleasant to hold (but doesn't like so much as to be possessive of it). A tennis ball could be a choice, for example. Have in your other hand a treat that your Boxer can't resist. Offer the ball to the Boxer. When she takes it in her mouth, say "*Take it!*" Now, offer her the treat as a swap, and say "*Give!*" or "*Out!*" when she drops the ball in your hand. Reward her with the treat. Repeat with all sorts of items sporadically through the day.

Keep highly valued items away: Often, a Boxer is possessive of a certain type of toy, a particular food item, or a specific item, such as a paper napkin. If you *know* your Boxer has a "thing" for a certain item, don't allow her to have access to this item. For example, if she is

good about all her toys except for a particular rubber crab, remove the rubber crab permanently from her toybox.

Teach your children: Boxers are generally terrific family pets and are exceptionally tolerant of children. That doesn't mean, however,

Destructive Behavior

If you're not sure when the destruction is occurring, set up a video recorder to capture your dog's activities after you've left. You might find out that she lies down and goes to sleep and becomes destructive only when she's bored.

that you should *expect* your Boxer to allow a child to reach into her mouth and yank out a toy or chew bone. If you have children, you must lay down the law: Do not take anything away from the Boxer, even if it's your toy! Come and get a parent.

In emergencies, swap items: If your Boxer has an item that you need to get out of her mouth immediately, use the *out* command. If your Boxer is not solid on this command, get a treat—or anything you can grab quickly that your Boxer might find yummy—and offer to make a swap with the dog. It's always better to remove the item from the dog's mouth without escalating the situation by directly confronting a guarding dog. Set your dog up to do the *right* thing by giving her a good choice (the treat). Then, work on teaching her the *out* command for any future instances.

Digging

If left unattended for any amount of time, a bored Boxer can dig trenches. The key to solving this problem involves two priorities. First, do not leave your Boxer unattended. If you are with your Boxer and she starts to dig, you can tell her, "*No!*" and redirect her to another activity (playing with you is usually a good choice). Second, exercise her more. Digging

Boxers, unless they've scented something underground, such as a vole or another exciting varmint, are usually digging out of boredom. Give the digging Boxer more exercise and she'll often be more content to relax during other times of the day.

Separation Anxiety

Boxers are a very devoted breed, and they love to be with their people. For some Boxers, the absence of their owners can cause moderate to severe anxiety. This is more than just the dog missing her owner. Dogs suffering from separation anxiety can become so frantic that they can be a danger to themselves.

Symptoms of a Boxer suffering from separation anxiety include increasingly agitated behavior as you prepare to leave the home, barking, whining, pacing, panting as you leave, and destructive behavior that begins within the first 30 minutes after you've left (i.e., chewing, ripping upholstery, urinating, defecating, scratching doors, clawing blinds, etc.).

Working with Separation Anxiety

If your Boxer is moderately distressed when you leave her home alone, there are several things you can do to help her become more relaxed and less anxious:

Mix it up: Boxers with separation anxiety look for cues that you are getting ready to leave. In fact, they most likely will know your routine better than you. It helps your Boxer if you can identify what types of things you do prior to leaving, and then do these same activities throughout the day *without leaving*. For example, pick up your car keys and then put them back down. Take out your jacket and

then put it back. Pull on your boots, pull off your boots. Open the front door and close it. Ignore anxious behaviors. Reward relaxed, calm behavior.

Consider safe confinement: If your Boxer thinks of her crate as a "safe" haven, consider crating her to minimize her destructive behavior.

Warning: If the Boxer is not crate-trained or is not relaxed in her crate, crating her will only elevate her stress level.

Increase her exercise: A tired dog is often a more relaxed dog. If she's sleeping, she's not stressing.

Consider pheromones: Dog Appeasing Pheromone or DAP is a product that is available as a plug-in that sprays the synthetic hormone on a timed basis. DAP simulates the pheromone that is produced by lactating dogs. Whether your Boxer is a puppy or an adult dog, she will recognize it as a soothing scent.

Prescription medications: In more severe cases of separation anxiety (in which the dog may injure herself), your veterinarian may feel your Boxer could benefit from a medication specifically designed to treat dogs with this anxiety disorder. The medications alone will not "cure" the Boxer of her separation anxiety; however, when combined with a desensitization program (picking up keys and setting them back down; rewarding good behaviors and ignoring anxious ones), many dogs can learn to relax while their owners are gone.

Be patient: Your Boxer does not choose to be terrified when you leave her alone; she just is. Work with her. Be kind. Be patient. She can become much more relaxed over time but it will take work.

TRAVELING WITH YOUR BOXER

One of the benefits to owning such a delightful, easily trained breed is that you can take the Boxer with you almost everywhere you go. Acclimating a Boxer to "all things travel" is not difficult; it just takes a little travel-savvy dog knowledge and practice.

Overcoming Motion Sickness

A common puppy problem is motion sickness. Theories abound as to why most puppies end up drooling and/or vomiting when riding in cars, but at the present time no one knows why for sure. Since most puppies outgrow their motion sickness by the time they are a year old (many outgrow it much sooner), it is plausible that the puppy's inner ear is not fully developed at a young age.

Whatever the reason, you may find that your Boxer puppy is a bit queasy on rides. The following are a few ways to help your Boxer until she outgrows this phase:

✔ **Use a crate:** If your Boxer puppy is comfortable in her crate at home, the same crate will serve as a security blanket in the car.

✔ **Keep it cool:** If you're having troubles keeping your Boxer's crate cool in the car, invest in a crate fan. They run on batteries and are quite effective.

✔ **Relieve your dog:** Make sure your Boxer has relieved herself before you put her in the car. Help her to be as comfortable as possible.

✔ **Exercise:** Try to make sure your Boxer has had a nice long walk prior to traveling in the car. A tired puppy will usually sleep.

✔ **Antianxiety aids:** If the source of your puppy's motion sickness is related to high anxiety, addressing her stress levels may help her overall comfort in the car. Rescue Remedy (a few drops on her gums) or Dog Appeasing Pheromone (DAP) may be of some benefit to the anxious Boxer.

True Motion Sickness

If your puppy does not outgrow her nausea when riding in the car, consult with your veterinarian for assistance. Your veterinarian may be able to prescribe medication that can help your Boxer feel more comfortable. Or, he or she may find an underlying problem that can be treated or managed.

Riding Securely

Perhaps the safest way for a Boxer to ride in a car is to ride in a crate. The crate should be large enough for the Boxer to stand up, turn around, and lie down. It should be well ventilated or have a crate fan for added air circulation. And, the crate should be fastened securely in the car so that it does not go tumbling if you brake suddenly.

Another option is a car barrier. If you have an SUV, you can have a pet barrier put in behind the last row of seats that effectively divides the passenger seats from the cargo area. The Boxer will have more room to move around and a nice soft bed can be placed in that area. If you are traveling any distances, you will not be able to put your luggage in back with your Boxer—for

the safety of your Boxer (sudden stops = luggage on Boxer) and your luggage (a great chew toy. Thanks, mom!).

If you want your Boxer to ride shotgun with you, a safe solution is a safety harness. These harnesses are padded and fit the Boxer snuggly. When attached to the existing seatbelt, the harness keeps the Boxer in her seat, but allows her to sit, lie down, stand, and turn around.

Good Manners

A Boxer with impeccable manners is a joy to travel with and is sure to score many car trips and travel opportunities. Before you take your Boxer on the road, there are a few commands and travel manners she should have mastered to make your trip more enjoyable.

At a minimum, your Boxer should be solid in her basic commands of *sit, down, come,* and *walk nicely* (see the chapter on basic training for more information on training these skills). In addition to these basic commands, there are a few other skills you can teach your Boxer that will make traveling even easier.

Hush

Inevitably after traveling for hours on end and arriving at a hotel, your Boxer will be full of energy. If you can't take her for a lengthy walk, sometimes this translates into a barky Boxer. To avoid having disgruntled lodgers call the front office to complain of the dog noise, be sure to teach your Boxer the *hush* command (see page 74).

Go Potty

When traveling, your Boxer may be limited to a very small patch of grass, or may need to

relieve herself on pavement. If you've trained your Boxer the *go potty* command (see page 32), you can encourage your Boxer to relieve herself virtually anywhere, anytime.

Wait Command

If your Boxer tends to bolt out of the car when you open the door, teach her the *wait* command. With the *wait* command, you can open the car door, the crate door, or a hotel door, and know that your Boxer will wait on the other side until you release her. The *wait* is different from the *stay* command in that the Boxer learns that she must remain in place momentarily.

There are many ways that the *wait* can be taught; however, here is one method that is relatively simple.

1. With your Boxer's crate inside the home, put your Boxer in her crate and shut the door.

2. Open the door slightly with your right hand held up in a *stop* position and say, "*Wait!*"

3. Shut the door, and reward your Boxer with a treat.

4. Repeat steps one through three several times before opening the door wider.

5. When you've finished your last repetition, give your Boxer a release command, "*Okay!*" and let her come out.

The Crate As a Comfort Zone

When staying in a hotel, you should never allow your Boxer to be loose in the room when you are not there. Many a dog has been lost when the cleaning services have opened a room door and a frightened canine has run out.

So, whether you use a crate at home or in the car, you should acclimate your Boxer to a crate and ensure that she is comfortable staying in the crate when no one is around. A Boxer that is not accustomed to being in a crate may bark when left alone. A dog that is barking in a hotel room is generally not a good thing and can lead to quite a few complaints.

Acclimating your Boxer to a crate is not difficult. First, make sure the crate is the appropriate size. It should be at least big enough for your dog to stand up without crouching, turn around, and lie down in a sprawled-out position. The crate may be wire, which is all open and provides excellent air circulation. Metal crates, however, can be quite heavy (something to keep in mind if you're lugging the crate up a flight of stairs) and though most varieties *do* fold for storage, they are still awkward to carry.

Or, your Boxer may prefer a plastic crate, which is more denlike. Plastic crates are quite lightweight, and they come in two pieces (top and bottom), which can be stacked in the rear of the car and filled with other luggage when traveling. They are still awkward to carry, however, and they do not provide the airflow that a metal crate would. You can help solve the airflow problem by purchasing a battery-powered crate fan.

Once you've chosen your crate, work to make it a positive experience for your Boxer. Feed her in her crate. Give her choice chew bones in her crate. Toss treats in her crate. Put a soft bed in her crate. Soon, she will be seeking out her crate for naps, meals, and treat time. When you travel with the crate, be sure to give her the same positive experiences—in her crate. She will be comfortable and secure whenever you have to leave your room.

6. When you are confident that you can open the crate door, give the *wait* command and your Boxer (no matter how excited she is) will remain in the crate; move the crate to the car or a more distracting environment, and continue practicing. This one command will be invaluable for those who travel frequently with their Boxers.

Go to Your Place

It's been a long day of driving, you've arrived at your destination, and your Boxer is jumping from bed to bed. You want to go to sleep. If your Boxer has ridden all day in a crate, you don't want her to have to sleep confined all night. Now what?

With the *go to your place* command, you can teach your Boxer to lie down and sleep virtually anywhere. The principle behind this command is to teach your Boxer to lie down and relax on a specific blanket or pad. You can then place the blanket anywhere, and if you tell your Boxer to *go to your place*, she will find the blanket and lie down.

To teach the *go to your place* command, start off simply.

1. Place the blanket on the floor next to you.

2. Put a leash on your Boxer.

3. Lure your Boxer onto the blanket (two paws is fine at first) with a treat.

4. Reward her with a treat.

5. Work to get all four paws on the blanket. Mark and reward the behavior.

6. When your Boxer gets completely on the blanket, then give the command, "*Place!*"

7. Continue to work linking the command "*Place!*" with walking over to and standing on the blanket.

8. As she links the command with standing on the blanket, start to move the blanket to different locations. At first, keep the blanket close by and gradually move it to across a room, up on a couch, or under a table. Make it a game to find the blanket!

9. Add the *down* to the exercise.

Also, place the blanket in places in which you *know* your Boxer enjoys relaxing. This will help to associate a relaxed *down* (and sleep) with the blanket.

Mind Your Manners, Too

When traveling with your Boxer, be a good ambassador for all pet-owning travelers. Obey hotel rules as to where your Boxer can and can't be, pick up after your Boxer, prevent any indoor accidents or destruction by using a crate when you can't be in the room, and be respectful of guests who don't love dogs as much as you do. Keep your Boxer on leash and close to you.

And, enjoy! Your Boxer will be able to see more areas of the country than she ever would if she had to be kenneled.

AGING BOXERS

With some thoughtfulness, advance planning, and a little flexibility, you should be able to maintain a high-quality of life for your graying Boxer.

Physical Changes

One of the most obvious changes that occur with American-bred Boxers is the overall graying of the dog's coat as he ages. For this reason, senior Boxers are often referred to as "Silver" Boxers. It truly is a beautiful sight to see a happy, healthy, and well-loved Boxer live to an advanced age.

Along with aging come a few physical changes. Some of these changes are inevitable; they're just part of growing older. Other changes may have a hereditary basis or may be a result of an earlier injury or disease. Regardless, when you note any changes in your Boxer, it is important to seek veterinary advice and care.

Though many age-related conditions cannot be reversed or cured, they can be managed. And, the most important thing to offer an aging Boxer is a comfortable, pain-free quality of life for his last years with you.

The following are several age-related physical changes that you are likely to encounter as your Boxer ages, as well as some tips to helping him maintain his health as well as possible.

Arthritis

If a dog lives long enough, he will at some point develop arthritis in one or more joints. Arthritis is inflammation in the joint, usually caused from wear and tear (normal or abnormal) on the joint. Dogs (as with humans) are born with cartilage on joint surfaces that provide natural cushioning. Over time, this cartilage wears away, becoming thinner or absent in areas. Moving on joints with little or no cartilage irritates the joint and in turn produces inflammation.

Mild cases of arthritis are usually fairly well tolerated; however, if the progression is not slowed, a severe case of arthritis can be crippling. Signs of arthritis include slight to moderate limping, inflammation (swelling) around the joint area, reactiveness to touch in the joint area, and a reluctance to rise from a lying down position or to jump up on furniture.

══ T I P ══

Treating Arthritis

Though at the present time there is no known way to regenerate lost cartilage and completely restore joints, there are several forms of treatment that can slow or ease your Boxer's arthritic pain. These treatments include joint supplements, nonsteroidal antiinflammatory drugs (NSAIDs) pain medications, and surgery.

If your Boxer is diagnosed with arthritis, discuss with your veterinarian *all* of your options, carefully weighing the pros and cons of the treatments.

Ways you can make him more comfortable include providing a soft comfortable bed, keeping his nails short, placing nonslip area rugs on slick floors, exercising him gently and regularly (swimming is wonderful!), and keeping him at a healthy, light weight.

Gingival Hyperplasia

The most common condition that occurs in the Boxer's mouth as he ages is gingival hyperplasia. With this condition, the Boxer's gums become enlarged and eventually envelope the teeth. In severe cases of gingival hyperplasia, surgery is necessary to remove excess gum tissue.

At present, the cause of gingival hyperplasia is not known, nor is there a means of completely preventing this painful condition. There is a way to slow the progression of the gum growth so that your Boxer may never require surgery: brushing your Boxer's teeth *regularly*.

It seems keeping the plaque, tartar, and gingivitis to a minimum retards the unbridled growth of gum tissue. Coupled with professional (veterinary) teeth cleaning on an annual basis, gingival hyperplasia usually can be kept in check.

Incontinence

Incontinence is generally an issue with spayed, often overweight (but not necessarily) females. Incontinence is different from "an accident" in that the Boxer does not know she is leaking urine. Usually, leaks occur when the Boxer is in a deep sleep. The leak may be very slight or it could be a large pool.

Do not blame your Boxer! She has no control over what has happened. Do take her to your veterinarian.

Managing Incontinence

If your veterinarian has diagnosed the problem as urinary incontinence (and ruled out other possible causes, such as a urinary tract infection, diabetes, kidney disease, or a thyroid condition), there are several things you can do to limit leakage:

✔ An overweight Boxer should be put on a weight reduction plan; excess weight puts pressure on the bladder, which in turn puts pressure on the urinary sphincter and can make incontinence issues more prominent.

✔ Exercise your Boxer. Strengthening your Boxer and helping her build muscle can help strengthen the muscles around the urinary sphincter, giving your Boxer more control.

✔ Keep her dry. Wrap the padding of her bed in a trash bag and then cover this with the regular bed cover. If she leaks, you can wash the bed cover and change the trash bag without destroying the inner bed padding. Hint: keep several bed covers of the same size so you can easily change a cover without waiting for the damp one to wash and dry.

✔ Keep her clean. Leaving urine on her coat not only smells but it burns her skin as well. If she wakes up wet, be sure to wash all urine-soaked areas with warm water and a mild shampoo.

✔ Seek veterinary intervention. If your Boxer's leaking is more than an occasional drip now and then, and has progressed to a real, household issue, ask your veterinarian about available medications. There are currently several prescription medications that have exceptionally high to complete success rates and have minimal potential for side effects.

✔ Surgical options. In some cases that don't respond to oral prescription medications, collagen injections have been used successfully to narrow the urinary sphincter.

Lipomas

These benign, fatty tumors look ugly but they are relatively harmless. Some Boxers have relatively few lipomas; others seem to be covered in them. The tumors start out small, but can grow to be the size of a golf ball or larger. They usually feel loose in the skin but if growing between muscle layers, a lipoma may have a more flat appearance. Lipomas are removed only if they restrict the dog's movement or cause him pain (for example, if a large lipoma was growing on the dog's chest and he couldn't lie down comfortably).

It is important to have every new lipoma checked by your veterinarian. Cancer is very prevalent in the Boxer, and you don't want to confuse a harmless lipoma with a potentially fatal cancerous growth. The diagnosis for a lipoma involves taking a sample of the tumor

Signs of Pain

Restlessness, panting, trembling, shaking, quick, shallow breathing, rapid heartbeat, crying, whimpering, limping, sensitivity to pressure or guarding of a certain body part, and refusing to eat or drink are more obvious signs of pain.

In addition, the American Animal Hospital Association recently released a list of six additional, but less obvious, signs of pain:
- Abnormal chewing habits
- Drastic weight gain or loss
- Avoidance of affection or handling
- Decreased movement and exercise
- Excessive licking, biting, or gnawing on himself
- Uncharacteristic "accidents" in the home

You know your Boxer best. If you feel he is ill or in pain, take him to your veterinarian for an examination. If he exhibits the odd behavior only occasionally, try to record the behavior on video and show your veterinarian what the Boxer is doing that's unusual. This can help in directing the veterinarian's attention.

with a needle (aspiration). Your veterinarian will be able to look at the sample of the tumor and confirm (while you're in the office) that the tumor is a lipoma.

Vision and Hearing

Sudden blindness or deafness is *not* a normal process of aging. Gradual decreased vision and hearing can be, however. Nuclear sclerosis, a natural, age-related clouding of the eye, can gradually reduce an aging Boxer's vision. Your Boxer's hearing may deteriorate over time and with aging, and you may find your Boxer sleeping through noises he would never have missed two or three years prior.

With vision and hearing, if you notice any signs of pain or discomfort, have your Boxer examined by your veterinarian immediately.

Mental Changes

Nearly one-third of all dogs aged 11 years or older show at least one symptom of cognitive dysfunction syndrome (CDS), with many dogs showing multiple signs. If you are lucky enough to have your Boxer live past 10 years of age, there is a significant chance that your Boxer may be faced with some loss of cognitive functioning.

Symptoms of Cognitive Dysfunction Syndrome

The early stages of CDS may present very vague symptoms or none at all. Later stages may present with many different and varied symptoms. The following are the four symptoms that are most commonly recognized as early signs of CDS: Changes in social behaviors, disorientation, interrupted sleep cycle, and loss of house-training.

Treatment of CDS

A lot remains to be learned about this condition; however, veterinary research is making gains every day. Current recommendations for treating CDS include

1. Special diet: Diets that are rich in antioxidants, such as alpha lipoic acid, beta carotene, and vitamin C, and contain fish-based omega-3 fatty acids, such as docosahexaenoic acid (DHA) and eicosapentaenoic acid (EPA) have shown to be helpful in improving cognitive abilities in older dogs.

2. Prescription medications: ANIPRAL (Selegiline hydrochloride, L-deprenyl) has been shown to temporarily reverse and improve CDS behaviors in some dogs within 30 days.

3. Mental stimulation: Mentally stimulating your Boxer on a regular basis seems to help slow the progression of CDS. You can get your Boxer's mind working by taking him for a daily walk, interacting with friendly dogs (i.e., a play group), and interactive toys, such as those that require him to work to remove a treat. Daily fun obedience training (nothing hard!) can help your Boxer's mind stay active, too.

Enriching the Senior Boxer's Life

The key in providing your Boxer with a continued, high quality of life is to keep him stimulated mentally and physically. Your Boxer is likely to be far less demanding in his advanced years for attention, so it's easy as an owner to not interact as much with him as you used to when he was a puppy. That's not the best tactic to take, however. As a senior, your Boxer requires just as much physical and mental stimulation as he did as a puppy—possibly even more—to maintain his physical and mental health.

Before you panic and feel as if you just got your Boxer to settle down (and now you have to go back to intensive puppy day schedule), it's not that difficult.

Exercise: If you've stopped taking your Boxer for daily walks, start back again! It doesn't have to be a power walk, run, or serious conditioning; your purpose now is to give your Boxer new sights and sounds to experience. You want him to use all his senses and stimulate as many areas of his brain as possible.

Make new friends: Socialization is a lifelong skill. If your Boxer enjoys going to the dog park, but is perhaps a bit more frail than he used to be, take him when there are only a few, gentle dogs present. Introduce him to new people on your walks. If your children are grown but your Boxer loved going to kids' soccer games, take him back to the games and let him make an entirely new set of little kid friends.

Touch him: Brush him, rub him, pat him. One of the highest rewards for a dog is to be physically praised.

Talk to him: It doesn't matter what the subject is, your Boxer enjoys the sound of your voice and the companionship.

Teach him something new: Old Boxers learn new tricks quite well, and he'll love the hands-on interaction with his favorite person in the world, *you*. Choose tricks that allow for any limited mobility.

Puzzle him: He'll love solving problems if the solution involves a bit of biscuit or peanut butter. Look for interactive toys that require the dog to do something for the toy to release food. It used to keep him busy as a puppy; now it will work those brain cells!

Love him: No one can tell you how long your beloved Boxer will be with you. Cherish every day of his final years. Make them the best they can be.

INFORMATION

Organizations

American Kennel Club (AKC)
5580 Centerview Drive
Raleigh, NC 27606-3390
(919) 233-9767
www.akc.org
E-mail: info@akc.org

Canadian Kennel Club
200 Ronson Drive, Suite 400
Etobicoke, Ontario Canada M9W 5Z9
(416) 675-5511
www.ckc.ca

The Kennel Club (United Kingdom)
1-5 Clarges Street
Piccadilly, London W1J 8AB
0844 463 3980
www.thekennelclub.org.uk

Fédération Cynologique Internationale
FCI Office
Place Albert 1er, 13
B-6530 Thuin Belgique
Tél: +32.71.59.12.38
www.fci.be

United Kennel Club (UKC)
100 East Kilgore Road
Kalamazoo, MI 49002-5584
(269) 343-9020
www.ukcdogs.com

Boxer Clubs

American Boxer Club (ABC)
www.americanboxerclub.org

United States Boxer Association (USBA)
http://p2.hostingprod.com/@usabox.org/ index.html

Boxer-Klub E.V. Sitz München
Vledener Str 64+66
81241 Munich, Germany
011 49-89-54670812
www.bk-muenchen.de/english.htm

Health Organizations

Canine Eye Registration Foundation (CERF)
Veterinary Medical DataBases-VMDB/CERF
1717 Philo Road
P.O. Box 3007
Urbana, IL 61803-3007
(217) 693-4800
www.vmdb.org/cerf.html

Canine Health Information Center (CHIC)
2300 E. Nifong Boulevard
Columbia, MO 65201-3806
(573) 442-0418
www.caninehealthinfo.org/chicinfo.htm

Orthopedic Foundation for Animals (OFA)
2300 E. Nifong Boulevard
Columbia, MO 65201-3806
(573) 442-0418
www.offa.org
E-mail: ofa@offa.org

University of Pennsylvania Hip Improvement Program (PennHip)
Veterinary Hospital of University of Pennsylvania
3900 Delancey Street
Philadelphia, PA 19104-6010
(215) 898-4680
www.pennhip.org

Breed Books

Tomita, Richard. *The World of the Boxer.* Neptune City, NJ: TFH, 1997.

Walker, Joan H. *The Boxer Handbook.* Hauppauge, NY: Barron's, 2000.

Walker, Joan H. *Training Your Boxer.* Hauppauge, NY: Barron's, 2001.

Clicker Training

Book, Mandy and Cheryl Smith. *Quick Clicks: 40 Fast and Fun Behaviors to Train with a Clicker.* Wenatchee, WA: Dogwise Publishing, 2001.

Pryor, Karen. *Click! Dog Training System.* (Book and clicker) New York: Metro Books, 2007.

Pryor, Karen. *Clicker Training for Dogs, 4th Edition.* Waltham, MA: Sunshine Books, Inc., 2005.

About the Author

Joan Hustace Walker is a member of the Dog Writer's Association of America (DWAA) and The Authors Guild. The author of 18 books and hundreds of articles, Walker has been nominated for 27 national awards, and has received the DWAA's coveted Maxwell Award six times, including the award for the 2006 Best Single Breed Book. Joan has been active in conformation, obedience, performance events, and rescue at various levels of participation for the past 30+ years.

Acknowledgments

This book would not have been possible without the help of many, many Boxer fanciers. In particular, I would like to express my gratitude to Tracy Hendrickson (Sunchase Boxers and founder of Boxer Rescue) for her kind and generous help, and her truly undying devotion to the "breed in need."

Important Note

This pet owner's manual tells the reader how to buy or adopt and care for a Boxer. The author and publisher consider it important to point out that the advice given in this book is meant primarily for normally developed dogs of excellent physical health and good character.

Anyone who adopts a fully grown dog should be aware that the animal has already formed its basic impressions of humans. The new owner should watch the dog carefully, including its behavior toward humans, and should meet the previous owner.

Caution is further advised in the association of children with dogs, in meeting with other dogs, and in exercising the dog without proper safeguards.

Even well-behaved and carefully supervised dogs sometimes do damage to someone else's property or cause accidents. It is therefore in the owner's interest to be adequately insured against such eventualities, and we strongly urge all dog owners to purchase a liability policy that covers their dog(s).

Cover Photos

Jean Fogle: inside front cover, inside back cover; Pets by Paulette: back cover; Shutterstock: front cover.

Photo Credits

Kent Dannen: pages 51, 75; Cheryl Ertelt: pages 2–3, 4, 18, 26, 37, 42, 56, 69, 76; Jean Fogle: pages 36, 49, 50, 54, 55, 58, 59, 60, 63, 64, 65, 67, 70, 71, 79, 83, 87, 91; Isabelle Francais: pages 9, 12, 15, 16, 20, 21, 23, 24, 25, 27, 28, 29, 34, 43, 44, 72, 77, 85; Daniel Johnson: pages 74, 82; Pets by Paulette: pages 5, 6, 11, 13, 19, 22, 30, 31, 35, 52, 53, 61, 66, 73, 81, 86, 93; Connie Summers/Paulette Johnson: pages 10, 80.

All inquiries should be addressed to:
Barron's Educational Series, Inc.
250 Wireless Boulevard
Hauppauge, NY 11788
www.barronseduc.com

ISBN-13: 978-0-7641-4326-7
ISBN-10: 0-7641-4326-3

Library of Congress Catalog Card No. 2009033223

Library of Congress Cataloging-in-Publication Data
Walker, Joan Hustace, 1962-
    Boxers : everything about purchase, training, feeding, and health care / Joan H. Walker
        p. cm.
    Includes bibliographical references and index.
    ISBN-13: 978-0-7641-4326-7 (alk. paper)
    ISBN-10: 0-7641-4326-3 (alk. paper)
    1. Boxer (Dog breed) I. Title.
SF429.B75W3615 2010
636.73–dc22   2009033223

Printed in China
9 8 7 6 5 4 3 2 1